bell hooks

A CRITICAL INTRODUCTION TO MEDIA AND COMMUNICATION THEORY

David W. Park
Series Editor

Vol. 8

The Critical Introduction to Media and Communication Theory series
is part of the Peter Lang Media and Communication list.
Every volume is peer reviewed and meets
the highest quality standards for content and production.

PETER LANG
New York • Washington, D.C./Baltimore • Bern
Frankfurt • Berlin • Brussels • Vienna • Oxford

CATHERINE R. SQUIRES

bell hooks

A CRITICAL INTRODUCTION TO MEDIA AND COMMUNICATION THEORY

PETER LANG
New York • Washington, D.C./Baltimore • Bern
Frankfurt • Berlin • Brussels • Vienna • Oxford

Library of Congress Cataloging-in-Publication Data
Squires, Catherine R.
Bell Hooks: a critical introduction to media
and communication theory / Catherine R. Squires.
p. cm. — (A critical introduction to media and communication theory; vol. 8)
Includes bibliographical references and index.
1. Mass media and race relations—United States.
2. Racism in mass media—United States. 3. Hooks, Bell. I. Title.
P94.5.M552U668   302.23092—dc23   2012042565
ISBN 978-1-4331-1587-5 (hardcover)
ISBN 978-1-4331-1586-8 (paperback)
ISBN 978-1-4539-1026-9 (e-book)
ISSN 1947-6264

Bibliographic information published by **Die Deutsche Nationalbibliothek.**
Die Deutsche Nationalbibliothek lists this publication in the "Deutsche
Nationalbibliografie"; detailed bibliographic data is available
on the Internet at http://dnb.d-nb.de/.

The paper in this book meets the guidelines for permanence and durability
of the Committee on Production Guidelines for Book Longevity
of the Council of Library Resources.

Contents

Preface

I first encountered bell hooks when I was an undergraduate living in Los Angeles, California, far from my midwestern home. In a feminist studies class, we read *Ain't I a Woman*, just weeks before the city convulsed into violent protests. A jury acquitted the white police officers who savagely beat Rodney King, captured on videotape, and the world turned upside down. bell hooks was one source of clarity I turned to as I tried to make sense of it all. I was frustrated and angered by the continual roll of the same images of looters on television, while few reports about the gang truce and other positive actions of community members made the front pages. If I knew anything, I knew I wanted to study more thinkers like hooks to help me understand these events.

It is uncanny that, at the 20th anniversary of those riots—uprisings, if you will—and in the wake of Mr. King's death, I have finished this book about bell hooks and Communication Studies. hooks, as much as any of my professors, inspired me to pursue a degree in this field, to investigate why and how our media systems continue to churn out so many hurtful images and distorted narratives with racist, sexist, classist undertones.

I am sure many scholars of my generation—and subsequent cohorts—could share similar stories of inspiration. Indeed, I was pleasantly surprised when I was invited to talk about this book and was greeted by a standing-room-only crowd of graduate students in gender studies. This crowd was notably more diverse than most I'd been part of in graduate school, and they asked sophisticated, often poignant questions about theories and current events. Their queries went far beyond the heated debates of the culture wars I'd been unwittingly tangled in when folks often dismissed hooks' work—or were still unaware of it—in many of my Communication Studies classes and some of the Feminist Studies courses.

It has been thrilling, and a privilege, to revisit bell hooks' work and think of her influence on myself and my field. Without hooks and her cohort of critical thinkers, our field would be poorly equipped to make sense of, and theorize, contemporary communication phenomena, let alone be reflexive about the motives and directions of our research and teaching practices. This book has provided me with an opportunity to examine my own habits, to revisit questions within the field, and to reflect on my own academic life. One moment of reflection was prompted unexpectedly as I literally lifted the cover of the book *Yearning* to rediscover an inscription written by my mother. She gave me the book as a gift as I began my graduate studies. The inscription wishes for me an intellectual life that will satisfy my yearnings, and I must admit I was teary-eyed as I read that wish, reflecting on how much of it has been granted, and how much more I've to discover.

— Catherine R. Squires
July 2012

Acknowledgments

I would be remiss if I didn't begin by expressing my heartfelt gratitude to Dave Park for inviting me to be part of this series. I thank him for his careful editing skills and his always-enthusiastic (often hilarious) right-on-time email communications over the process of drafting this book. While all errors remaining are certainly due to my faults, Dave has been a wonderful editor from start to finish. I hope to join him on some future project.

All writers depend on a community for sustenance, and mine has been rock solid. Many thanks to the members of the Faculty of Color Writing Group who provide me with incentive to "show up" for the work, and with fabulous camaraderie to boot. Thanks also to the Office for Equity & Diversity at the University of Minnesota for supporting our group for the past two years. To my family and friends in Saint Paul, Evanston, Washington, D.C., Chicago, Tempe, and Ann Arbor, kudos for the well-timed emails, phone calls, Facebook and face-to-face pep talks. To my twins, Will and Helena, and my life partner, Bryan, your love and understanding are priceless to me.

I presented some parts of this book to the University of Minnesota Gender, Women's & Sexuality Studies department colloquium, and work influenced by it at Arizona State University. I appreciate the warm welcome and substantive feedback I gained from each visit, and hope I did justice to the suggestions I tried to incorporate.

To close, a deep thanks to bell hooks, who continues to contribute to our most urgent debates about democracy, justice, and fairness. One book cannot do justice to the breadth and depth of your work, but I do hope that this volume provides readers in Communication Studies with a spark of the inspiration you gave me when I needed it.

one

An Introduction to bell hooks

Students, especially younger ones, may have a hard time engaging with bell hooks' early, generative works, due in part to at least two factors. First, hooks began writing at a time that may seem distant and strange: the 1980s and 1990s sparked many cultural and political controversies that continue to shape our society today, but the era may be obscure to today's graduates and undergraduates. Second, hooks has been faulted by her critics for not following traditional academic writing and research procedures. Indeed, she often does not use traditional footnotes or internal citations, nor delineate her methods in a fashion consonant with conventional research papers. One of the main goals of this book, then, is to translate her work, so to speak, for audiences more familiar with conventional academic writing. This opening chapter also aims to situate hooks in a wider historical context, providing background for readers without direct experience of the socio-political environment in which her work emerged. The book aims to present and discuss her work in a way that illuminates long-debated questions about media and society, and pose and re-frame questions about media, identity, and social justice.

This chapter begins with a brief biography of bell hooks (née Gloria Watkins), and then proceeds on a compressed tour of the cultural and political landscape from which hooks' work emerged. This is not to suggest that hooks' work is anachronistic or that she is more of a historical figure, but rather to provide readers with sufficient context to better understand the impetus for her theories and to engage with her practice of weaving together personal reflections, pop culture references, and stories. The chapter sets the scene through a mix of biography and cultural history. This provides some background for the debates about the nature of scholarship, power, and identity that figure in hooks' writings about communication, representation, and power. I hope the introduction's format facilitates readers' engagement with her approaches to media and society.

From Gloria Watkins to bell hooks

Gloria Watkins was born in Hopkinsville, Kentucky, on September 25, 1952. Raised by her parents and grandparents, she attended segregated schools as a young child, and experienced the everyday politics and indignities of racism and sexism. Importantly, though, she remembers the efforts her elders, teachers, and other community members made to instill a sense of dignity and purpose in her and the other children. On top of this, as a child and young adult, she was witness to, and beneficiary of, the resilience and resistance that gave rise to the direct action movements that dismantled Jim Crow. She came of age during the civil rights movement, bused to the high school that used to be all-white, as she and her classmates formed the vanguard of desegregation.

Although her home life was not idyllic, she writes often about how loved she felt by members of her family, how much care she experienced under the tutelage of dear schoolteachers and neighbors.[1] Young Gloria Watkins imbibed the cultural richness of her community; even though most of the people were poor in terms of monetary wealth, she experienced the bounty of aesthetic and spiritual resources in the homeplaces she visited, in school performances, and in the games she played with her sisters and friends. Told repeatedly at a young age by her parents that she talked back too much, she seized on stories about her grandmother, bell, whose spirit someone recognized in Gloria when she spoke her mind. She recounts in many writings and interviews that she chose the alternate name "bell hooks" to honor her grandmother.

When I was a child, when I would speak harshly back to adults—talk back—they would say to me, you must be bell hooks' granddaughter. . . .

I've written so much about that sense of coming from a legacy of outspoken women, because certainly my mother's mother was a very outspoken woman. And that sense of that being a natural part of who I am.[2]

The outspoken child and voracious reader left Kentucky to attend Stanford, graduating in 1973 and moving on to the University of Wisconsin, where she earned her master's degree in 1976. She later completed her PhD at the University

---

1. See bell hooks' discussions of her childhood in *Outlaw Culture: Resisting Representations; Bone Black: Memories of Girlhood*, amongst other writings.
2. "In Depth with bell hooks." CSPAN Video Library. http://www.c-spanvideo.org/program/InDepthw

of California, Santa Cruz, in 1983, two years after she published her landmark book, *Ain't I a Woman: Black Women and Feminism,* under the pen name bell hooks. The pseudonym and its lowercase spelling are used, she explains, to put the focus on the writing, not the identity of the writers. With this volume, hooks became part of another vanguard: black women writers whose feminist vantage points complicated and enriched an intellectual landscape heretofore dominated by white men, black men, and white women. hooks' cohort soon found their work and personas interwoven with multiple strands of political and cultural controversy and breakthroughs as the 1980s unfolded.

bell hooks and the 1980s: Culture Wars and Questioning Political Identities

Many of today's popular, nostalgic looks back at the 1980s are riffs on big hair, shoulder pads, neon, and iconic MTV videos. What is less often recalled in these fond memories of the decade are the contentious fights over the direction of American culture and politics that raged across a host of institutions, often highlighted (and distorted) on proliferating cable television channels. When *Ain't I a Woman* was first published, the terms "affirmative action baby," "racial resentment," "political correctness," "post-feminism," "do-me feminism," and "post-racial" were not yet in wide circulation or causing tempests in media teapots. But the 1980s spawned these and other contentious terms in the often raucous and uncivil debates in academic and other spheres about the changing natures and roles of media, education, and group identities in our society.[3] hooks' writings have touched on all of these areas, launching into academic and lay discourses an incisive, fiercely worded diagnosis of the ways that American history and white-dominated feminist academic circles had failed to take into account Black women's experiences.

The interest in and controversy surrounding *Ain't I a Woman* coincided with rising public interest in Black women writers. At the same time that novelists Toni Morrison (*Beloved*), Alice Walker (*The Color Purple*), and Terri McMillan (*Waiting to Exhale*) were becoming famous, Black feminists were writing cultural theory and criticism in the academy and getting attention well beyond the ivory tower as they challenged the Euro-centrism of many feminist and cultural studies texts. Books such as Michelle Wallace's *Black Macho and the Myth of the Superwoman* and activist scholar Angela Davis' *Women, Race & Class* were often interleaved with copies of *The Bluest Eye* and *The Color Purple* on bookstore and living room shelves. Like the other women listed here, hooks became a media star, one of the

---

3. See also Faludi's *Backlash: The Undeclared War Against American Women*; Dillard's *Guess Who's Coming to Dinner Now?;* Kelly's *Yo' Mama's Dysfunktional! Fighting the Culture Wars*; and Vavrus' *Postfeminist News* for thorough summaries and reflections on the wide-ranging and contentious fights over the meaning of feminism, race, and social progress that occurred in the media.

"black public intellectuals" of the 1980s and 1990s who were implicated in, and called upon to prosecute, the "culture wars" over art, public education, and the growing influence of Black artists on mainstream popular culture.

Black women writers and their allies were not merely questioning their exclusion from the "canonical" texts of history, literature, and social science; this was a clarion call to awaken scholars to the fact that their ignorance of Black women's lives and contributions was a fatal flaw to "universal" theories of gender and society, race and political power, identity and culture. As such, writers such as hooks were in conflict with conservative cultural gatekeepers who argued that the canon should not be disturbed; to do so would unravel American civilization and devalue core beliefs in merit, individualism, and competition.

Obviously, hooks was not alone in her diagnosis of academic theories and commercial cultural products that universalized whites as normative subjects. Scholars such as Kimberle Crenshaw, Stuart Hall, Derrick Bell, Judith Butler, and Iris Marion Young delineated how prior scholarship and theory had failed to interrogate how the perspectives of people of color, gays and lesbians, women, and so on, complicated the grand narratives of Family, Nation, Beauty, or Love. And their contributions were met with a fierce backlash across the political spectrum, a backlash that was highly visible in mainstream political debates and cultural productions as well as at "the margins" of society. Indeed, hooks and her colleagues were part of a wave of intellectuals who not only benefitted from the end of racial segregation and gender exclusion in terms of access to academic spaces formerly the realm of white men, but also demanded that their presence be something much more than set decoration. They aimed to profoundly transform institutions and cultural practices.

Debating the Import and Impact of Black/Feminist Identities

hooks and her fellow intellectuals began their careers at a time when many people across different spheres of society—politics, art, science, media—were asking, what does it mean to be Black? Or: Is feminism still necessary? In the wake of the triumphs of the civil rights and feminist movements, the end of *de jure* inequality, and, allegedly, the end of "second class citizenship," was it still necessary to think of "black culture" or even blackness, as a way to categorize people, experience, expression? Did women need to band together against patriarchy after Title IX and *Roe v. Wade*? The 1980s were a decade that brought incredible change to mainstream U.S. media's representations to race and gender, even as inequalities persisted in multiple spheres.

As Nelson George put it in his collection, *Buppies, B-boys, Baps and Bohos*, during that decade, "the black aesthetic (a term that refers not just to music but to a whole way of being). . . evolved with blinding speed."[4] And, as his title suggests, the salient, visible range of black identities was multiplying, with many representations of this "post-soul" Black generation on network and cable TV. In the midst of these changes, new Black stars were made. From Michael Jackson's rewriting of the record books for pop sales to Eddie Murphy's avalanche of comedy films to Tina Turner's comeback, African American celebrities reached levels of fame and wealth unheard of in prior decades. Rap and hip hop became targets of fierce moral debates even as the genre became a cross-over cash cow for the music industry. The firestorm over rap—particularly its most graphic and violent "gangsta" formats—threatened to obscure the political possibilities that emerged from Black and Latino youth acquiring publicity and voice through music.

Even though economic and social disparities were clearly implicated in many of the new black representations, the emergence of so many new images and narratives had no clear connection to a new black politics, particularly when contrasted with the direct action and legal strategies of the 1960s. What did it mean to have so many visible, popular, and wealthy black people at the same time that the culture wars raged about affirmative action and hip hop? What was the political role—if any—for the new generation of black celebrities who benefitted so greatly from the gains of the movement? As exemplified by basketball phenom Michael Jordan's refusal to endorse a black U.S. Senate candidate from his home state, Black celebrities and media representations were not easy to identify in terms of politics, relationships to Black communities, or to classify as "positive" or "negative." New identifications and ways of being in the growing multi-media structure were emerging, and many debates occurred over people's sense of what it meant to be Black in post–civil–rights America. bell hooks, along with Henry Louis Gates, Jr., Cornel West, and others, were viewed as the go-to public intellectuals for this question. In their books, speeches, and popular articles, these scholars contributed to the country's fitful discussions of race matters, theorizing how, and to what extent, Black life had changed in the wake of the civil rights movement and legal changes.

At the same time that blackness and African American celebrity culture were put under the microscope, similar scrutiny was applied to feminism and women's identities. The term "post-feminist" came into vogue in discussions of allegedly failed—or obsolete—feminist strategies. Reports that the generation of women and girls who benefitted mightily from Title IX weren't interested in calling themselves feminist were rampant, as were references to divisions in the movement caused by different perspectives on the import of sexuality, class, and race in women's lives. In these debates, hooks' name and work was often invoked alongside a handful of other black feminists such as Angela Davis or Michelle Wallace. Too

---

4. George, *Buppies, B-boys, Baps and Bohos*, xi.

often their names were used to suggest a failed feminism's disunity; other times they were mis-aligned with retrograde black female writers such as Shahrazad Ali, or had any positive references to heterosexual romance classified as "do-me feminism."[5] What got lost in the shuffle was the complex, sometimes subtle, yet powerful, arguments that race, gender, and class are interlocking systems, that we see the world and our experiences through the prism of multiple facets of identity, not single ones. What got lost in the titillating dissection of "do-me feminism" were the ways in which different feminist perspectives had always existed; their progenitors just rarely got noticed or got full attention from either scholars or the media.

The public, wide-ranging discourses of race, gender, class, and sexuality were churned up by a media machine looking for hot stories. Although hooks and her colleagues often interjected brilliant deconstructions, not only of theory, but also of its misuse in popular media accounts of the culture wars, many people have been left with little sense of the actual ideas and interests articulated in the pages of the books whose provocative titles were easy to throw in for good measure in a controversial story. It is important to return to these debates and to revisit how bell hooks and others unraveled the conservative assumptions of the dominant discourses, discourses which we still live with today. Echoes of the 1980s and 1990s were easy to hear, for example, when pundits and politicians declared Democrats had "abandoned women" when the party nominated Barack Obama over Hillary Clinton. We can see that the lessons of intersectionality haven't reached many quarters when these kinds of arguments are made that suggest white women are the only women, or that women somehow "choose" between their gender and their race when thinking about political candidates.

Clearly, our need for thinkers such as bell hooks has not lessened when we reflect on the state of mediated discourse in the U.S. But because she has been a participant (or implicated) in many of the most contentious debates about media, identity, academia, and society, some have shied away from her work. Indeed, she is often noted as a provocateur, and has been criticized for using an unconventional writing style. Some scholars have publicly excoriated her work as academically unfit. For students and faculty who are not familiar with her, their first introduction to hooks may come from hearsay, and the controversies that have surrounded her work and persona may hinder engagement with her work. Her insistence on grounding her theoretical and critical insights in standpoint, with attention to power and history, and her willingness to explore connections between individual and group experiences, have produced provocative, but fruitful, conjectures about

---

5. For example, in 1994, an *Esquire* magazine writer classified bell hooks as a "do-me" or "pro-sex" feminist alongside writers such as Katie Roiphe, with whom hooks has little in common theoretically or politically. Indeed, hooks devoted a significant chapter in *Outlaw Culture* to critique Roiphe's approach to acquaintance rape and her shallow, middle-class-centered views on feminist politics.

media and culture. Likewise, her discussions of how social location shapes ability to "see" or "not see" racism, sexism, or classism in the media, and her determination to illustrate how our choices implicate us in systems of power, provide models for scholars and students engaged in humanistic inquiry into media texts and audiences. As such, this book seeks to offer readers a measured, contextualized introduction to her work, and to illustrate how her work on media and culture still speaks to many key concepts and questions in Communication Studies as well as to ongoing debates in our culture.

The next chapter, "Deconstructing Dominator Culture," outlines bell hooks' philosophies about representation, identity, critical thought, and power. Chapter Two attends to the centrality of standpoint theory to hooks' theoretical work, and her insistence that critics be self-reflexive about their motives, knowledge, and experiences as they engage in the study of media and society. The chapter maps the roots of her intellectual work: her upbringing in the Jim Crow South, her spiritual engagement with Buddhism, and her discovery of radical pedagogy scholars such as Paolo Freire that shaped her views of social transformation. The third chapter then turns to descriptions of how her writings resonate with the work of traditional scholars who are more often linked to Communication Studies: John Dewey, C. Wright Mills, and Jürgen Habermas. For example, many of hooks' writings meditate on moving between black and white segregated spaces as well as media offerings, illuminating and embodying themes of multiple, overlapping public spheres, and the role of media in shaping the limits and quality of citizen exchange and political debate. Likewise, her concerns about the power of media to shape our psychological, political, and cultural orientation to the world resonate with calls for scholars to employ their knowledge to revitalize education and community formation.

Although hooks' autoethnographic and experimental writing may not, at first glance, seem to offer much to traditional media research, her insights challenge students and scholars to reexamine and expand their research questions, their objects of study, and to consider our own agency and responsibility as we investigate how media impacts our world. The fourth chapter, "Media, Power, and Intersections," lays out bell hooks' contributions to explorations of the power of the mass media. Importantly, like other contemporary black feminist theorists, hooks grasps the importance and influence of media images and narratives of marginalized groups. But, unlike much early media criticism of African American portrayals that focused on whether texts were "positive" or "negative," hooks brought a more nuanced approach, layered with considerations of political economy, social psychology, and interpersonal communication. Through a focus on her film and television criticism, the chapter delineates how hooks opens doors for other scholars who seek to understand multiple facets and origins of raced and gendered media representations, and how these facets reflect on varied aspects of individual and social experiences. The chapter also contains examples of work by other communication scholars who have been influenced by her approach.

The fifth chapter turns to media audiences through the themes of reception, resistance, and recovery. Chapter Five shows how hooks' work demonstrates the ways in which marginalized people interact with pop culture every day, and illuminates strategies for resistance and analysis of dominant media. Her attention to how marginalized groups interact with media also reveals blind spots in conventional theories of spectatorship. Crucially, hooks pushes against the romanticization of the scope and impact of *individual* acts of resistant reading or critical engagement with media. She calls on scholars and lay community to leverage these "everyday acts" to spark communal forms of resistance and production of counter-hegemonic media. The chapter considers the label "cultural critic," the most common nomination applied to hooks, and one she uses herself. Here, I describe hooks' understanding of the role of cultural critics in educating audiences. hooks believes that progressive cultural criticism is part and parcel of transformative politics, and that critics must position themselves to share their knowledge and cultivate criticism in a wider conversation with the public. Moreover, she locates spaces for learning cultural criticism not only in academia, but also in media spectatorship.

Many readers either overlook or dismiss her insistence on linking pleasurable/critical media interactions to politics. At the end of the chapter, I suggest we consider her popular publishing—particularly her children's books—as part of a larger project of making black feminist, non-violent media more widely available to challenge status quo renderings of the world and our places in it. In this way, she is hoping to provide, through mass publishing, media texts born of the type of criticism she conducts, and media texts that, hopefully, convey an image of a just, inclusive world in a pleasurable way—just as the media she critiques package violence and exploitation in pleasurable forms.

For communication scholars who teach courses on media and social change, media and politics, or interpersonal communication, hooks presents a clear challenge to reexamine whether our pedagogy reinforces or replicates the same patterns of domination we critique in media. The sixth chapter, "Education As a Tool for Democracy," engages her call to remake our classrooms. For students, her discussions of the dynamics of the classroom may seem strange, or off-topic for media studies. However, when reading some of hooks' more controversial exhortations regarding passion, pop culture, and teacher-student relationships, it behooves us to attend to the core message: If we want our students, or broader reading audiences, to understand the importance and impact of media, we cannot inspire them to take a more critical stance unless we engage them with passion and care. Thus, in this chapter I consider hooks' call to extend our critiques of media and power to reexamine our relations with colleagues and students, and the ways in which her understanding of standpoint theory expands our ability to engage in productive dialogues about media and society. While some readers are discomfited by her seemingly radical extension of the feminist tenet "the personal is political," her deep commitment to applying lessons from analyses of power and representation to our practices in public and interpersonal interactions is provocative and, for those engaged in teaching topics that intersect with her *oeuvre*, intriguing. In the concluding section, I revisit the main topics of the previous chapters and suggest areas of research and practice that hooks' work continues to speak to, decades after the publication of signature works such as *Ain't I a Woman* and *Black Looks: Race & Representation*.

two

Deconstructing
Dominator Culture

Every citizen in a dominator culture has been socialized to believe that domination is the foundation of all human relations.[1]

bell hooks is concerned with liberation. As the opening chapter explained, her work is directed toward facilitating anti-racist, anti-sexist transformations through democratic education and cultural criticism. She is committed to making connections between theory and everyday life. She is particularly concerned that theories of democracy, freedom, communication, or aesthetics are worth little if scholars do not explain how to put theory into everyday practice. Writing in *Teaching to Transgress,* she posits that theory isn't inherently "liberatory or revolutionary. It fulfills this function only when we ask that it do so and direct our theorizing towards this end."[2] Readers who are new to her work might initially be startled by her blunt declaration of the political utility of theory. Many courses on communication theory or other social theories are taught from the perspective of objectivity, suggesting that the theorist or social scientist should not have any skin in the game—her or his theories should emerge from disinterested inquiry into a particular phenomenon with no goal other than to understand the relevant variables and possible outcomes. In contrast, hooks, like other critical cultural theorists, has a clear objective: to provide citizens with liberatory insights into our culture, and theoretical tools that will not only help us understand our predicament,

---

1. hooks, *Teaching Community,* 75.
2. hooks, *Teaching to Transgress,* 61.

but also lead to transformative action. This means creating theories and practices that upend racism, sexism, homophobia, and class exploitation. Her goal is communicated quite clearly in the titles of her books: *Killing Rage, Ending Racism*; *Teaching Community: A Pedagogy of Hope*; and *Teaching to Transgress: Education as the Practice of Social Freedom*. These titles do not beat around any rhetorical bushes: they tell prospective readers right away that she believes we have much to learn and un-learn to achieve the freedoms lauded in normative definitions of democracy, enlightenment, multiculturalism. As a corpus, hooks' work outlines a philosophy of liberation set in contrast to the hegemonic ideology of domination.

Throughout her writings, hooks refers to our hegemonic culture as a "dominator culture." Indeed, if one were asked to give a sound bite to describe the aim of her work, one might say hooks is seeking means to transform dominator culture into liberatory culture. bell hooks serves up a tall order, by any measure, and one that may not immediately strike readers as part of Communication Studies. But she operates like other philosophers and theorists who provide large-scale analyses of society, turning to historical comparison, detailed observations, and cultural critique to make a diagnosis and suggest remedies for a range of interrelated social ills that intersects with issues central to Communication Studies.

This chapter outlines hooks' philosophy with attention to key terms, problems, and approaches addressed in her body of work. I summarize hooks' understanding of power and inequality, viewed from the standpoint of Black feminist thought, critical cultural studies, and Buddhism. Taking multiple strands from these schools of thought, hooks weaves together a compelling and provocative vision of how we might re-configure our society through transformations of our material and spiritual environment. Central to her vision are considerations of: the uses and abuses of power; essentialism; dialogue; community; imagination; intersectionality; and the uses of history. Here, I will relate how she and other black feminist theorists use intersectionality, autoethnography, and historical recovery of Black women's voices to theorize resistance and alternatives to dominator culture.

Defining Dominator Culture

We live in a world in crisis—a world governed by politics of domination, one in which the belief in a notion of superior and inferior, and its concomitant ideology—that the superior should rule over the inferior—effects the lives of all people everywhere.[3]

The hegemonic "dominator" culture hooks defines and deconstructs is that which arose in the West in the age of colonialism and racial slavery. Like other critical

---
3. hooks, *Talking Back: Thinking Feminist, Thinking Black*, 19.

theorists of gender, race, and post-colonialism, hooks understands this dominator culture as an outgrowth of the violent, exploitative form of imperialist capitalism that formed strict racial and gender hierarchies as part and parcel of social organization, labor extraction, and legal status. She insists upon using the term "white patriarchal capitalist supremacy"[4] to define this specific historical formation of dominator culture in the United States. To make explicit the role of white supremacy in dominator culture is not to essentialize whiteness, or condemn all white people as rabid racists, past, present, and future. Just like Black people will occupy different identities and responses to dominator culture, white people are diverse in terms of class, gender, etc., and can exercise agency within white supremacist culture. In many essays hooks relates stories of white allies and students who have worked hard to resist white supremacy and unlearn its insistence that blackness is inferior. Rather, she is describing the system in terms of which group has gained the most privilege, highest status, and amassed the most power over others.

hooks chooses to use white supremacy rather than "racism" to describe how the hegemonic dominator culture is built in part on the "exploitation of black people and other people of color," partly because of the dilution and ubiquity of the word racism in contemporary discourses of multiculturalism.[5] Specifically, hooks suggests that "racism" has become over-articulated with individual prejudices in common, and much academic, parlance. Individualized, racism has lost its connection with the role and forms of institutional and structural practices that reproduce racial inequalities and reinforce white privilege across a host of socioeconomic, political, and cultural domains. Thus, it is easy to turn a blind eye to how one might reinforce racial inequality even if one does not consciously hold or express racist opinions. hooks also asserts that using "white supremacy" is more suited to describing both the continuation of white privilege and "the way we as black people directly exercise power over one another when we perpetrate white supremacist beliefs" now that civil rights reforms have made it easier for people of color to "ally themselves politically with the dominant racist white group."[6] Whereas anyone, regardless of group identity, can hold racist beliefs, hooks wants us to understand the systemic as well as the interpersonal dynamics of racial hierarchy.

Transforming Dominator Culture

Most Communication Studies scholars acknowledge that cultures are not static, but active and multifaceted. Culture permeates our lives, and structures our habits of mind, our assumptions and expectations about ourselves and others. Working

---

4. See hooks' discussion and definition of this and other terms such as racism and sexism in *Talking Back; Yearning: Race, Gender and Cultural Politics*, especially Chapter 1, "Liberation Scenes," and Chapter 6, "Critical Interrogation: Talking Race, Resisting Racism."
5. *Talking Back*, 112.
6. Ibid., 113.

in the critical cultural studies paradigm, hooks posits the co-existence of multiple cultures within a nation-state, one which is hegemonic but contested. Although the hegemonic group's culture is positioned as normal, justified, and superior to others, cultural hegemony is never total; there are always spaces and moments of resistance. Although the dominant culture and political system positions the hegemonic group as subjects—people with agency to define themselves and act upon the world—and subordinate groups as objects—people without agency who are acted upon by others—there are always spaces for subordinate groups to practice resistance and act as subjects. Crucially, even members of oppressed groups have agency in some limited contexts. It is imperative for members of those groups to foster oppositional thought, to participate in alternative cultures, and to build community with each other to develop tactics to sustain resistance. Where dominant culture views subordinate groups as objects, oppositional thinking helps subordinate groups reject that disempowered position.

An important component of asserting subjectivity is "moving from silence to speech. . .a gesture of defiance that heals, that makes new life and growth possible. . .the expression of our movement from object to subject."[7] Clearly, communication across a number of contexts is central to this movement from silence to speech. In hooks' estimation, we empower ourselves, we gain self-determination, when we are able to speak from our experiences and stand in common struggle with allies against domination. Sometimes counter-hegemonic thoughts and actions are visible, sometimes not. But to understand how to resist the hegemonic culture and its related socio-political manifestations, one must accurately describe and deconstruct its practices, assumptions, and processes of reinforcing the status quo. The role of cultural studies, then, is to investigate how, where, and in what ways specific people can resist hegemony and transform dominator culture into a culture that better reflects the ideals of democracy and personal freedom. As subordinate groups, such as Black Americans, assert their agency and take control of their self-definition, chances improve for engagement in "subject to subject contact between white and black, which signals the absence of domination, of an oppressor/oppressed relationship."[8] But such interaction can only "emerge through mutual choice and negotiation."[9]

By approaching dominator culture as a system where people of marginalized and dominant identity groups interact, struggle, and negotiate power, hooks pushes against hegemonic discourses that focus on individual-level phenomena as the drivers of hierarchical social outcomes. Its component parts articulate which groups and ideologies have structured, and benefit the most from, the current state and form of our politics and culture. Including patriarchy and capitalism in her

7. Ibid., 9.
8. hooks, *Outlaw Culture: Resisting Representations*, 28.
9. Ibid.

description of dominator culture, she reminds us to apply intersectional analysis to our understandings of power. It is insufficient to theorize about how dominant cultures oppress particular groups without attending to how multiple axes of identity intersect and inform each other. By insisting that we examine race, gender/sex, and class simultaneously, she pushes readers to disengage from other normalized aspects of dominator culture: individualism, essentialism, and binarism.

Individualism

One of the central assumptions of white supremacist capitalist patriarchy is the primacy of the individual and his/her quest to wield power and status over others. Individual material gain within the capitalist system—even at the expense of others—is celebrated.[10] Individualist values are viewed positively across a host of legal, social, and cultural texts, and communal mores are suspect. Discourses of meritocracy obfuscate the ways in which class and other social categories come to hinder individuals' ability to garner resources to compete in the capitalist marketplace, reinforcing the myth that if someone is not successful, she only has herself to blame. Individualism encourages people to think of themselves as separate entities, like the atomized rational individual of some economic theories. This concept of a self that is radically separate from Others can lead to alienation and spiritual emptiness, even when its adherents amass personal wealth and power. She declares, "Addiction to materialism knows no class,"[11] and discusses with Cornel West in *Breaking Bread* the widespread feelings of emptiness expressed by people who have "made it" in terms of financial gain, but who feel depressed and alone.

hooks draws upon two main resources to argue against, and provide an alternative to, the dogma of individualism: (1) communal values she learned and experienced as a child in a community of anti-racist resistance that are evident in many aspects of Black cultures; and (2) Buddhist philosophy and practices. Key here are concepts of mutuality, respect, and communion. hooks underscores, through classroom memories, family anecdotes, and meditations on Buddhism, that we do not go through the world as islands, but as engaged, interactive members of communities large and small. There are joys and benefits we experience only through community ties. When we are engaged in mutually supportive efforts and understandings of each other, we can feel connections and garner strength from them. When black people (or others) turn to dominator values, they lose the ability "to understand or appreciate. . .the importance of mutual interdependency, of communal living. . .that we collectively shape the terms of our survival."[12] Importantly, people can experience the love, camaraderie, and support of community

---

10. *Talking Back*, 30.
11. hooks, *Salvation: Black People and Love* (New York: Harper Perennial, 2001), 11.
12. hooks and West, *Breaking Bread*, 10.

without material wealth. Reflecting on her spiritual practices, which reinforce the value of being present-oriented and thinking deeply, she observes that people socialized in dominator culture are encouraged to be "geared toward the future, the perceived rewards that the imagined future will bring," and are discouraged from fully immersing themselves in their relationships, activities, the arts, in favor of plotting upward mobility.[13] This future orientation does not encourage habits of mind that open up the pleasures of contemplation, dialogue, attentive listening, and stillness, which sustain intellectual vibrancy and cultivate deep community ties. A present-oriented approach provides more space for us to experience learning or art or relationships as intrinsically valuable, rather than just a means to personal gain or material profit.[14]

Investment in the present tense does not require one become a monk, and fostering community does not mean separatism or group-think; rather, in resisting dominator culture, communities should necessarily make room for dissent and difference to leaven discussions and engender new ways of seeing the world. As bell hooks said in one dialogue with Cornel West,

> For too long we have conceptualized the Black community in narrow terms. We conceptualized it as a neighborhood that is all Black, something as superficial as that. When, in fact, it seems to me that it is by extending my sense of community that I am able to find nourishment.[15]

This kind of community is formed not by policing its borders to judge who is "really black." It sustains individuals through solidarity and acceptance of differences, always providing a homeplace to which one can return and recover oneself. Moreover, this "beloved community" hooks envisions prepares its members to engage with others based in "an ethic of relational reciprocity, one that is anti-domination," even as it recognizes that ongoing white supremacy requires people to "remain awake and vigilant everyday in our lives whether confronting people of color who have internalized racism or in all white settings where it is likely that many of those present have not unlearned racism."[16] She insists that we avoid making "blanket assumptions. . .about every white person we encounter. The reverse holds true for white people."[17] In seeking mutual dialogue, there is risk, but if we fail to believe change is possible, we inadvertently strengthen dominator culture by denying ourselves hope. As such, it is imperative to deconstruct essentialist approaches to identity so that we can imagine how malleable people's identities, as well as their attitudes and beliefs about race, gender, and class, could be.

---

13. hooks, *Teaching Community,* 165–67.
14. Ibid., 173.
15. hooks and West, *Breaking Bread,* 91.
16. hooks, *Belonging: A Culture of Place,* 87, 86.
17. Ibid., 86.

Essentialism and Binaries

Another aspect of dominator culture is its investment in essentialist binaries, or what hooks refers to as the "western metaphysical dualism" that undergirds the philosophy and logic of domination.[18] Exploitation of Othered groups is justified on the logic of binaries of identity that posit essential traits for each group on either side of the power line: Black/White; male/female; gay/straight; working class/middle class; each group is imagined as having different characteristics, abilities, and is thus deserving of different power positions. The binaristic approach of dominator culture not only asserts essential differences between groups, but also that groups on opposite sides of the binary occupy inferior/superior positions to each other. Anyone socialized in the white supremacist system is likely to view whiteness as pure, good, and civilized; blackness, as the binary opposite of whiteness, then, comes to represent everything that negates whiteness: soiled, evil, and savage. Likewise, the male/female binary is structured in ways that naturalize particular gender roles and the hierarchical valuation of masculine over feminine traits.

Binaries can affect the structure of oppositional thought. Members of oppressed groups may internalize either/or thinking and call for a reversal of polarity rather than a holistic transformation of the culture. Remaining within the binary "common sense" that one group will dominate an Othered group makes it difficult to imagine anti-essentialist options for political alliances or cultural production. Moreover, those members of dominant or oppressed groups who have internalized this way of thinking "may feel threatened by any critical approach that does not reinforce this perspective" (*Yearning*, p.8). Hence the need for sustained critical education and continuing dialogues that offer alternative ways of envisioning society, interpersonal relations, and group identities. These dialogues are, in some ways, part of the process of de-essentializing identity and thinking outside of the proscribed either/or frameworks of dominator culture in order to see the ways of understanding identity and power through a both/and approach.

Binaries don't operate only to define identity groups; binary thinking infuses other realms of thought and institutional organization. Dualism also frames our experiences in compartmentalized ways. For example, within the dominant Western intellectual tradition, mind and body are distinct; intellectual matters are separate from spiritual matters. hooks was drawn to Buddhism when she entered university in part because she found in it a holistic approach to spirituality and intellectual life that resonated with her investment in the mystical forms of Christianity that had imbued in her the understanding that spiritual experience "transcends both authority and law."[19] As she struggled to unify her intellectual, political, and spiritual practices, the teachings of Trungpa Rinpoche and Thich Nhat Hanh inspired her.

18. hooks, *Yearning*, 8.
19. hooks, *Teaching Community*, 161.

Hanh writes of self-recovery. In the Buddhist tradition, he says, people used to speak of enlightenment as a kind of returning home. "The three worlds," he says, "the world of form, of nonform, of desire, these are not your homes." These are places you wander off to. . .alienated from your true nature. So enlightenment is the way to get back: the way home. . . I began to use this vision of spiritual self-recovery in relationship to the political self-recovery of colonized and oppressed peoples.[20]

These and other Buddhist writers helped hooks resist the pressure to segment her life in the academy, and to reject forms of anti-racism that depended upon a still-dualistic revision of the already-existing racial system, where Blackness was promoted as both profoundly different from, and superior to, whiteness. From her engaged Buddhist practice and learning, she realized a form of engaged pedagogy to teach students not only to resist the dominant culture's call to segment their lives, but also to limit the scope of their ability to identify with others of any background.

Rather than question why a Black woman should be a Buddhist, and be concerned with the suffering of Tibetans when there is still work to be done to defeat racism in the U.S., hooks' reply is that it makes perfect sense for Black people, who have found joy in struggle and have survived and generated beauty even as they suffered deeply, to be drawn to "a spirituality based in the premise that all life is suffering."[21] Moreover, she asserts that Buddhism's questioning of dichotomies teaches her that "my being is connected to the being of all those toiling and suffering Tibetan people. . . . That connection is part of our understanding of compassion: that it is expansive, that it moves in a continuum."[22] Rather than lay out the world in terms of essential identity boundaries that dictate the limits of our empathy, hooks explains that she can be committed to both Tibetan and Black resistance to domination without seeing it as a zero-sum game of loyalty or resource allocation.

The both/and approach suggests ways to challenge essentialism and to engage people perceived or defined as Other without resorting to assumptions about their "nature" or essential political investments. This opens up space to imagine solidarity with a range of people not based in shared identity, but in shared commitments and concerns. Importantly, both/and thinking also suggests the need to re-think binaries that separate "private" and "public" experiences, necessitating a closer examination of how psychological/personal and social/public issues may be interrelated. The notion of suffering and compassion recall that the marginalized are not the only ones who yearn for a different socio-political environment. In this shared yearning, hooks theorizes, space can be created for real, earnest

20. Ibid., 161–62.
21. Ibid., 176.
22. Ibid., 159.

dialogue, solidarity, sharing, and transformation for members of dominant and oppressed classes. Communicating with others about this yearning, sharing ideas and experiences, and, importantly for media, creating visions of alternatives, are all-important components of resisting domination and making change. These activities prepare the way, so to speak, for new social formations, habits of mind, ways of seeing. One crucial habit of mind is developing the ability to understand intersectionality.

Intersections of Power and Identities

hooks suggests we conceptualize dominator culture as a matrix within which different groups are arrayed in overlapping, interlocking hierarchies of privilege and oppression. All of the groups have been shaped by—and to some extent deploy—the ideological frameworks of domination. Each group, and individuals within the groups, experiences the matrix of domination in different, yet related, ways. Thus, we need to attend to the intersections of identities, the ways in which specific categories of identity operate with and against each other to shape experiences within the system of dominant culture. Like other black feminist theorists, hooks' work demonstrates how attention to our multiple identities garners deeper understanding of how power operates, as well as shining light on the means for, and limits of, intergroup dialogue and solidarity.

Intersectionality, sometimes referred to as standpoint theory, posits that we can learn more about systems of power and oppression when we analyze race, gender, class, and other identity categories as part of an interlocking system of social hierarchy. Black feminists do this by centering black women's experiences, theorizing from the specific ways in which gender, class, sexuality, and age all contribute to how domination structures the lives and life chances of Black women. Importantly, intersectional analysis from Black feminists emphasizes that the matrix of power and identity is not all-encompassing; rather, Black women and other oppressed peoples have theorized resistance and alternative habits of mind from their specific standpoint. To this end, Patricia Hill Collins notes:

> Black women's actions in the struggle or group survival suggest a vision of community that stands in opposition to that extant in the dominant culture. The definition of community implicit in the market model sees community as arbitrary and fragile, structured fundamentally by competition and domination. In contrast, Afrocentric models of community stress connections, caring, and personal accountability.[23]

---

23. Collins, *Black Feminist Thought*, 221.

Intersectional analysis is sometimes misunderstood as "cultural relativism," where each individual's standpoint is just as good or valid as another. This is not the point of black feminist thought. Intersectional analysis is brought to bear to better understand how knowledge claims are related to systems of power, and how identities aren't additive. Again, I turn to Patricia Hill Collins:

> The existence of Black feminist thought suggests another alternative to the ostensibly objective norms of science and to relativism's claims that groups with competing knowledge claims are equal. . . . This approach to Afrocentric feminist thought allows African-American women to bring a Black women's standpoint to larger epistemological dialogues concerning the nature of the matrix of domination. Eventually such dialogues may get us to a point at which, claims Elsa Barkley Brown, "all people can learn to center in another experience, validate it, and judge it by its own standards without need of comparison or need to adopt that framework as their own." In such dialogues, "one has no need to 'decenter' anyone in order to center someone else; one has only to constantly, appropriately, 'pivot the center.'"[24]

The result of each pivot is not merely that we can appreciate how people see things differently, but that by considering the myriad views we actually learn more and can better assess the ways unfair inequalities are generated from socially constructed understandings of difference and unequal practices that reinforce power and resource imbalances.

Intersectional analysis is not only brought to bear on analysis of oppressor/ oppressed relationships. Many of hooks' essays attend to how the intersections of class and race, gender and race, internally affect Black communities and Black political struggles. These are important interventions, because hooks insists on pointing out how dominator culture has shaped certain habits of mind and being within many Black families and communities. For example, she points out how class mobility in the post–civil–rights era has allowed some Black people to gain greater economic agency. Many of these people have then supported exploitative elements of capitalist culture. This development of greater class segregation within the Black population can weaken solidarity with poorer Black people alongside. "To protect their class interests, [black elites] often make it seem as though black capitalism is the same as black self-determination. . .[and undermine] a vision of collective well-being that necessarily requires sharing skills and resources."[25] Intersectional analysis, then, is useful for multiple explorations of power and identity across a range of communities and situations, not just when the oppressed comment on the most dominant oppressor.

---

24. Collins, 236.
25. hooks, *Salvation*, 11.

The Personal Is Political

In addition to being structured along axes such as race, gender, and social class, the matrix of domination is structured on several levels. People experience and resist oppression on three levels: the level of personal biography; the group or community level of the cultural context created by race, class, and gender; and the systemic level of social institutions. Black feminist thought emphasizes all three levels as sites of domination and as potential sites of resistance.[26]

For hooks, resistance, like identity, is multifaceted, with personal and social components. How we imagine and strive for a good life, for happiness, is bound up and partly determined by the cultural, political, and economic systems in which we are embedded, as is our capacity for imagining alternatives. This requires us to understand the intersection between private and public experiences. Our imaginations, our aspirations, and our experiences of pleasure are part of the cultural practices and narratives that need to be examined as we resist dominator culture. As she wrote in *Yearning,*

All too often our political desire for change is seen as separate from our longings and passions that consume lots of time and energy in daily life. Particularly the realm of fantasizing is often seen as completely separate from politics. Yet I think of all the time black folks (especially the underclass) spend just fantasizing about what our lives would be like if there were no racism. . . . Surely our desire for radical social change is intimately linked with the desire to experience pleasure, erotic fulfillment, and a host of other passions.[27]

It is crucial, then, to consider the role of desire and pleasure-seeking in maintaining or resisting domination. We need to ask, how does dominator culture "look" appealing to people, even those who are most damaged by its practices? Media content that reflects the mores of domination make it look normal and good. Consumer capitalism and individualism suggest particular routes to happiness, fulfillment. Acquiring more and more goods is key to happiness, even if it means exploiting others to do so. Dog-eat-dog competition for wealth is presented as a tantalizing battle between winners and losers: losers are portrayed as individuals without the right stuff; winners are attractive and well-prepared to reap rewards. Bending others to your will is the stuff of heroes and heroines; subordinate groups are put in their place, having been shown to be not only inadequate in comparison to dominant groups but also happier occupying a lower status. The late Marlon Riggs catalogued in his documentary *Ethnic Notions* how for decades Hollywood portrayed African Americans as happy to be slaves or servants, making music or food for white folks' pleasure. Those who try to achieve better status

26. Collins, *Black Feminist Thought*, 222–23.
27. *Yearning*, 12–13.

are represented as failing, or are punished for trying. As I will discuss in Chapter Three, hooks delineates how the basics of domination are glamorized in film and television, transmitted through fairy tales and song lyrics. From romance novels that depict women happy to be "ravished" by tough, stoic male suitors, to gangsta rap lyrics that declare "pimps up hos down," patriarchal domination is portrayed as the way things are—and the way women really like it.

We know that organized groups have protested cultural narratives that reinforced gender hierarchy and racial inequalities. But for hooks, these oppositional expressions of conscience are only the beginning. "In that vacant space after one has resisted there is still the necessity to become—to make oneself anew."[28] That is, it is insufficient to protest particular representations and not offer alternative ways of being/seeing ourselves. For example, one's rejection of Hollywood's over-representation of Black servitude is not radical if all we require is to move, say, a black actress from the role of maid to that of the lady of the house. This desire to be "on top"—to occupy the dominator role rather than the dominated—does not destabilize the larger system of domination that makes relations between domestic workers and their employers so exploitative. While making the lady of the house a Black woman addresses some racial stereotypes, it alone doesn't address the power dynamics of race and class identity construction that normalize women of color as domestic help. This lone Black lady is the exception to the rule. Until we demand to see a maid (of any color) not just as the object of her mistress' commands, but depicted as a full human being with thoughts and desires of her own, we haven't undermined the status quo understandings of race/class/gender. When we put the domestic worker at the center of the story, we might be able to more easily see the asymmetrical relations of power that unnecessarily restrict her prospects and pave the way for her employer to maximize potential. If the maid is fully humanized, and is not there only to help the lady of the house fulfill her own desires, then we will have shifted our vision and found something truly new.

Critical Interventions in Dominator Culture

Culture is not monolithic, and cultural changes come not only from "progress" in technology or artistic invention, but also from contact—and sometimes conflict—with other cultures. For hooks, this latter aspect of cultural change is of prime interest: how does one resist a culture of domination when one is a member of an oppressed group within the society? The answer, in part, is to theorize from one's location using intersectional analysis drawn from experiences with the power structure. Such resistance is not an individual endeavor: it requires education, dialogue, opportunities for observation and reflection, and the creation of

---

28. Ibid., 15

communities that foster and sustain alternative habits of being and practices of critique.

Confronting the depth and complexity of culture and human agency, hooks understands that cultural transformation is a long-term project, with no guaranteed outcomes. She chides those who believe the legal reforms that resulted from social movements of the mid-twentieth century were sufficient to make gender and race equality a reality. Consider for a moment that for over 200 years a brutal regime of racial hierarchy shaped U.S. culture, citizen identities, and consciousness. With this in mind, we must consider the possibility that the mid-century civil rights reforms in the U.S. are still too new to have wiped out all inequalities and cultural proclivities born of racism. Even if the most aggressive proposals for change had been enacted—and by many accounts the U.S. has taken a much more conservative path to racial justice without even considering reparations.[29] Forty years is not enough time to jettison such deeply rooted sensibilities. We must acknowledge not only that there is still need for more legal, economic, and political reforms, but also that we must make conscious efforts to unlearn the cultural lessons that we have been taught for so long: that racial/gender difference, hierarchy and so forth, are "natural" ways of organizing and experiencing human life. Moving from a society where patriarchal domination and racial apartheid were the norm to a society that is anti-racist and anti-sexist requires us to create ways of being that promote and sustain new visions of multicultural, interdependent civil life. In some ways, hooks suggests, it is "easier" to theorize race under legal oppression, because of the stark lines drawn between peoples, places. There are clear rules of engagement. As she wrote in *Teaching Community*, "Segregation simplifies; integration requires that we come to terms with multiple ways of knowing, of interaction."[30]

Because particular oppressive tactics and habits of being—including modes of communication—sustained segregation, it is imperative to name, deconstruct, and un-learn those practices that structured and reinforced the racist, sexist, classist system. Dominant ways of seeing and understanding identity groups built up in that system were not legislated away in the Civil Rights Act of 1964 or washed away in the anti-colonial revolutions that swept Asia and Africa after World War II. The massive changes that these movements engendered created grounds upon which people can discover and practice ways to see, hear, talk about, and represent our humanity that are not determined by the assumptions of dominator culture. Theorizing from the perspective of the oppressed rather than the dominator class allows us access to perspectives and strategies to remake, or as hooks would say, recover, ourselves. hooks encourages us to understand how the legacies of the past affect our present as well as how we map out the future, and demands that we look

---

29. See, for example, Marable, *Race, Reform and Rebellion*.
30. hooks, *Teaching Community*, 78.

at the past with new eyes and new agendas for learning lessons. One important means for accomplishing this goal is to draw upon the experiences of oppressed people who resisted domination. Using history, memory, critical ethnography, and cultural criticism, hooks excavates tactics not only for resistance, but also for social transformation and spiritual recovery. "Theorizing black experience, we seek to uncover, restore, as well as deconstruct, so that new paths, different journeys, are possible."[31]

In nearly all of her books, hooks makes at least a brief mention of the rural, working class black community and family environment of her youth. That community provided her with the first stirrings of critical thinking, aesthetic awareness, and sense of agency she cultivated throughout her life. As a child, she witnessed and participated in conversations where Black adults scoffed at and deconstructed the images of black inferiority—or the absence of blackness—offered in films and television. She recalls her own pride and comfort attending then-segregated public schools and churches. There, Black teachers and leaders empowered her with self-esteem and rigorous standards for public speaking, and she experienced the pleasures of affirmation when she mastered and performed poetry, speeches, and plays. In her later work, she discusses in more detail how her grandfather was a model of nurturing Black manhood in contrast to the over-valuation of dominant, stoic patriarchs in white and Black culture. Her grandparents provided a vision of how a heterosexual black couple need not mimic the nuclear, patriarchal conformity of white middle class television fantasy. Rather, her grandparents' union was a "blend of togetherness and autonomy that is needed in healthy relationships,"[32] not subservience of woman to man. And she recounts feeling love and care even when material comforts were not readily available, emphasizing that a sense of community and wholeness is necessary to sustain people so that when the dominant culture devalues them, they can come home to a community that helps repair the damage.

This is not to downplay the impact of poverty or legal injustices; rather, hooks wants to elevate in our consciousness the importance of the ethic of caring as a bulwark against dominator culture's dismissal of caring as weakness. In order to resist dominator culture, one must be able to imagine alternatives to it. As she said in a dialogue with Cornel West, she often tells her students, "If you can't imagine something, it can't come into being."[33] Excavating through history, biography, and personal narratives the communal values that sustained black communities in times of extreme racist violence and legal oppression is one way to leaven our imaginations to foster ways of being that counter the dehumanizing effects of dominator culture. hooks suggests that the production of counter-memories pushes back against

---

31. hooks, *Black Looks: Race and Representation*, 172.
32. hooks, *Salvation*, xvi.
33. hooks and West, *Breaking Bread*, 110.

dominant histories that erase communities of color or downplay oppression in ways that help us, as Jonathan Arac wrote, "to understand and chance the present by placing it in a new relation to the past."[34] For black people to theorize about their community's experiences of white supremacy or other forms of domination is key to resistance because, as Edward Said wrote, making a concrete theory moves us toward consciousness and self-realization, "which of course is the revolutionary process stretching forward in time, perceivable now only as theory or projection."[35] Creating an "archaeology of memory" is part of building theories that "make return possible" to a place—the past—that is not home, but that we need to reinhabit and understand in order to make plans for the future.[36]

Unfortunately, there has not been sufficient discussion and interrogation of these values and their role in resistance. As discussed earlier, we must acknowledge that members of oppressed cultures often assimilate or amplify certain aspects of dominator culture. hooks diagnoses the depletion of the Black liberation movement's energies as partly due to a turn away from caring and nurturance, as well as a refusal to grapple with the toll of sexism and classism on Black community activism. Although there are black men and women who use feminist thought in struggle and solidarity, all too often black political movements are portrayed and structured through framework of patriarchy. This encourages the continued erasure of women's contributions to social movements and deprives men and women of the insights of black feminist thought, queer black thought, and other liberatory ways of seeing the world. She insists that until men can draw upon anti-sexist as well as anti-racist paradigms, they will not be able to "dream about masculinity that humanizes" rather than masculinity that dominates.[37] Without such dreams, it will be difficult at best to rebuild effective organizations and strategies for change without again making one fatal mistake of past movements: ignoring the effects of internal hierarchies and oppressive behaviors on communities of struggle.

Where Did the Love Go?

hooks does recognize that many black people were despairing and frustrated as the movement was attacked, its leaders targeted for assassination and its tenets described as dangerous, communist ideology. The seeming failure of non-violent resistance to create enough lasting change was too much for some to bear, while others argued that non-violence was always destined to fail, and more "realistic" tactics were necessary to win freedom. "After the slaughter of radical black men, the emotional devastation of soul murder and actual murder, many black people

---

34. Quoted in hooks, *Killing Rage, Ending Racism*, 45.
35. Quoted in *Killing Rage*, 41–42.
36. *Killing Rage*, 42.
37. hooks, *We Real Cool: Black Men and Masculinity*, 144.

became cynical about freedom. They wanted something more tangible, a goal that could be attained."[38]

An intersectional approach helps us see how institutions and practices within oppositional cultures can, in some contexts, actually reinforce domination or disable critique. hooks' chronicle of the end of the civil rights movement acknowledges the role of state violence, white backlash, and too little too late policy proposals. However, she turns a sober eye on the philosophical dynamics of the movement and how some Black leaders and laypeople seemed to abandon many of the habits of being that sustained the movement. Just as importantly, as they enacted anti-racist resistance, they often turned a blind eye to the ways in which sexism and classism were suppressing black people, draining much needed innovation and energy. Overlooking the ways gender and class contribute to racial oppression, fewer voices spoke out about, or theorized on, patriarchy, capitalism, or homophobia's role in domination. hooks boldly asserts that part of the movement's downfall was the failure of leaders to take on the challenge of dismantling multiple lines of oppression in order to further advance toward Black liberation. An enduring liberation movement, she argues, must address the fact and consequences of the internalization of certain tenets of dominator culture.

Likewise, hooks is concerned that the competitive individualism that is normalized in dominator culture, laid over gender hierarchy, encourages hurtful conflict amongst black men and women. For example, she and Cornel West discussed the surge of successes for black female writers in the 1990s and the subsequent debates of whether black women were benefiting at the expense of black men. She noted that "The myth that black women who succeed are taking away something from Black men continues to permeate Black psyches. . . Since capitalism is rooted in unequal distribution of resources, it is not surprising that we. . . find ourselves in situations of competition and conflict."[39] Internalizing the binaristic, individualistic understanding of success—a zero-sum game where the woman's achievement means failure for the man—creates a corrosive form of competition. This normalized, internalized battle of the sexes requires an intervention: the alternative viewpoints that intersectional analysis provides. Looking at the publishing world through the lens of black feminism, and thinking of the accomplishments of black authors over the last century, one can re-frame contemporary publishers' interest in black women writers. Notice that Black women writers have long been boxed out of the mainstream publishing business due to sexism and racism; notice that a multitude of Black voices in the marketplace of ideas will complicate and, hopefully, elevate discourses of race, gender, and class; and understand that black writers of both genders can support each other and engage

---

38. Ibid., 15.
39. hooks and West, *Breaking Bread*, 13.

in critical dialogue about each other's work without trashing each other in ways that reinforce harmful stereotypes and delay understanding.

hooks' analysis of the flaws of black freedom movements rests in part on a distinction between assimilation and liberation. Assimilation is what dominant groups expect of subordinate groups: Admire us and become like us—if we let you. Assimilation does not require the dominant group to give up or alter its cultural norms. Thus, black people who assimilate into white dominant culture will not rock the boat much and will be rewarded for accepting the status quo. This requires black people to conform "to a white, privileged class norm" instead of working "to transform the very definition of being, integrating a new model where difference is valued, adaptation is the goal."[40] Assimilation does not require the creation of an "environment in which people can hold all the differences and allow for harmony and dissent at the same time."[41] When Black people are compelled to (or agree to) assimilate into white culture—to exhibit the cultural habits and adopt the assumptions and perspectives of white culture—there is little destabilization of the anti-black tenets of white supremacy.

> Embedded in the logic of assimilation is the white supremacist assumption that blackness must be eradicated so that a new self, in this case a "white" self, can come into being. Of course, since we who are black can never be white, this very effort promotes and fosters serious psychological stress.[42]

Liberation, in contrast, comes when individuals can engage in an equal exchange of ideas without shame or fear. Liberation of oneself or one's group is not dependent upon conquering another group or excluding others from the group. In a true liberatory democracy, hooks writes, people of different cultural backgrounds, sexual orientations, religious tradition, etc., live in an atmosphere of mutual respect and recognize their inter-related interests. Individuals are not compelled to conform to the specific rules and guidelines of a specific culture, only to operate in the spirit of mutuality. hooks' vision resonates with philosophers of cosmopolitanism, such as Kwame Anthony Appiah, and feminist models of pluralism such as those articulated by Iris Marion Young.[43] Cosmopolitan and pluralistic societies recognize diversity as a source of innovation, strength, and a reflection of the constant flux of culture and history. hooks draws upon Judith Simmer-Brown's definition of pluralism and its distinction from diversity: "Diversity is a fact of modern life. . . . Pluralism, on the other hand, is a response to

---

40. hooks, *Talking Back*, 67.
41. hooks in conversation with Gary Olsen, "bell hooks and the Politics of Literacy," 6–7.
42. hooks, *Talking Back*, 67.
43. See Appiah, *Cosmopolitanism: Ethics in a World of Strangers*; Young, *Justice and the Politics of Difference*.

the fact of diversity. In pluralism, we commit to engage with the other person or the other community."[44]

Pluralist societies require attention to group differences and respect for individual freedoms, as well as effective mechanisms to foster interaction and understanding within and across group boundaries. Transforming a dominator culture—wherein our governmental structures and political practices continue to generate outcomes that deny mutuality and the humanity of many groups—into a liberatory society envisioned by hooks is a breathtaking goal. hooks is a normative theorist; she conveys aspirational models for crafting habits of mind and being to develop a just society. These habits of mind, she believes, were under-appreciated and under-utilized toward the end of the civil rights movement, contributing to its collapse.

In hooks' reckoning, too few black leaders continued to mine the habit of being critical of capitalism and its part in exploiting Black labor; too few fostered awareness and critique of sexism; too many turned toward "black capitalism" and material success as a benchmark for liberation, for progress. Dignity via money and power subsumed dignity via shared struggle and caring. She discusses this turn across multiple volumes, pointing to debates in black arts and literature as evidence of growing concern about Black values. hooks identifies Lorraine Hansberry's *A Raisin in the Sun* as a prescient warning that African Americans were soon to face what critic Margaret Wilkerson terms a struggle between "human values of integrity. . .and human worth measured by dollars."[45] The character of Walter Lee embodies this choice, anguished over whether to use the windfall from his father's life insurance to buy a liquor store—thereby profiting from the addiction of other Black people—or to buy a home and save for the further education of his younger siblings. In the end, Walter embraces the values represented by his mother, who asks him, "Since when did money become life?" hooks also finds evidence of concern about a coming tide of materialism in the writings and speeches of Martin Luther King Jr. and Malcolm X. While neither had fully grappled with their own sexism yet, both had launched fierce critiques of consumerism—what King called "hedonistic materialism"—and its potential to undermine Black community spirit as well as democratic reforms. Individualist capitalism does not foster cross-class solidarity and understanding; it accelerates and deepens competition for scarce resources. Placing one's faith in material wealth disconnects one from the joys of community and the strength found in pursuing mutual goals.

This more "tangible" goal—material gain—dovetailed with another goal: Patriarchal power. In white supremacist patriarchal capitalism, men are supposed to be breadwinners, to get ahead in the market to gain more power. For black men under slavery and Jim Crow, patriarchal power of this kind was rare, as most black

---

44. Quoted in hooks, *Teaching Community*, 47.
45. hooks, *We Real Cool*, 16.

men were not only denied opportunity in the marketplace, but were also brutalized physically and psychically by the impunity enjoyed by white men, who could
enter their homes, rape, steal, or kill, and never face punishment. Any black man
who retaliated, particularly in the South, was destined for lynching. Thus, hooks
writes, many black men equated liberation with patriarchal domination of women
and children—attaining the same powers enjoyed by white men. And, of course,
hegemonic culture reinforces the notion that men attain masculinity via providing for their families and being the head of the household, a seductive vision of
nuclear-family stability and wealth. But hooks finds that many men discover that
the promise of patriarchal power is hollow, particularly for Black communities,
given the exploitative capitalist system and the corrosive effects of gender hierarchy.

Shared experiences with racism can only take Black men and women of different classes, sexual orientations, and educational backgrounds so far. Plans for
action and visions of the future will necessarily differ across these other categories of identity. So too for women of different race, class, or sexualities. She explains this in the process of airing her frustrations with those white feminists
who continue to speak about and theorize the category "woman" as if there is an
essential female perspective and/or experience. Even with the common goal of
ending sexism, people will have "divergent perspectives on how that goal might
be reached. . .very different differences in experience, perspective and knowledge
make developing varied strategies for participation and transformation a necessary agenda."[46] She gives the example of two women who share the experience of
spousal abuse who might build feminist solidarity around that experience. However, if the two women are of different racial or class status, "not only would the
social construction and expression of femaleness differ, so too would their ideas
about how to confront and change their circumstances."[47]

In contrast to theorists who are vexed by the existence of multiple perspectives and the need to work through differences as part of social justice movements,
hooks is clear in her belief that only through engaging differences can better strategies be crafted to transform society. Clearly, the limitations on anti-racist struggle
that failed to grapple with class or gender hierarchy have reaped a harvest of tense
relationships and mistrust between Black men and women, and white feminists
and women of color, who must craft more robust alliances. hooks asks us to recognize how differences and commonalities emerge within diverse groups, both of
which can "enrich rather than diminish" our sense of what to do as we struggle
against patriarchy or racism or homophobia.[48] Only through mutually respectful
dialogue can this mix of common goals and varied experiences develop strategies
that won't replicate the imbalances of dominator culture. It may be painful at times

46. hooks, *Talking Back,* 23.
47. Ibid.
48. Ibid., 24.

to be part of these dialogues, but they are necessary to ferret out under-appreciated ideas and overlooked issues that will surely come back to haunt the community if they are not understood, reflected, and acted upon in common struggles.

Recovery and Love As Part of Liberation and Democracy

bell hooks is clear that these dialogues are best accompanied by individual reflection and healing of the psychic wounds inflicted by racism and sexism. She exhorts us to not minimize the impact of dominator culture on all of our psyches, our souls, and how the impact creates a ripple effect through communities and across generations. She urges everyone to aim for "self-recovery," to heal the wounds inflicted by dominator culture. Reflecting on her own process of self-recovery and models of self-recovery she has learned from or discovered in Black literature, autobiographies, and Buddhist spiritual teachings, she articulates why this self-healing process is profoundly political:

> I began to use this vision of spiritual self-recovery in relationship to the political self-recovery of colonized and oppressed people. I did this to see the points of convergence between the effort to live in the spirit and the effort of oppressed peoples to renew their spirits—to find themselves again in suffering and in resistance.[49]

The link between experiences of spiritual renewal, spiritual wholeness and yearning for justice, and political renewal provides hooks with another way to make connections between the personal and the political. It also suggests another set of memories and habits of being to use as contrasts to practices ingrained in dominator culture.

Theorizing from Experiences

Some have responded with disdain to bell hooks' divulgences of her Buddhist spirituality and her belief that psychological healing is a necessary element in social change. But recall her investment in the adage "the personal is political"; she conveys a clear-eyed understanding that the empowerment requires work, practice, and social organization. Spirituality and psychological recovery, then, are embedded in the context of returning to community ready to engage in conversation, struggle, and transformation such that one does not re-invent the wheel of domination. One can grasp how personal struggles are related to broader political and social phenomena more easily, perhaps, if the theoretical tools are situated in everyday experience and resonate with one's desire for spiritual renewal, for community.

hooks is critical of some feminist and some Black liberation scholars for not clearly laying out for broad audiences how their theories might help people access tools for self-recovery. She notes that women who are not exposed to how femi-

---

49. hooks, *Teaching Community*, 161–162.

nist thought can help them improve their lives often turn to self-help literature in magazines and books, "which offer models for personal change applicable to everyday life."[50] Ironically, the feminist movement has stimulated many desires amongst women for better lives, for empowerment, but feminism has become, in hooks' assessment, too inaccessible and bounded by academe for most women. Into this vacuum flow books such as *Women Who Love Too Much*, a bestseller because women do yearn for better relationships, fairer division of labor at home, and other ground-level experiences of equity. But these books rarely acknowledge "political realities, the oppression and domination of women" that make these advice regimens limited and limiting. Feminists need to ask themselves why women are returning to "narratives that suggest we are responsible for male domination,"[51] and they need to recognize that the failure to provide accessible alternative models of self-recovery is a political one that needs remedy. She calls on academics to be more active in translating their work and thinking about theory and praxis for broader publics. As I will discuss in a later chapter, this critique of ivory-tower-bound theory extends through her writings on education and media literacy, as well as challenges to the ways in which even liberal scholars reinforce dominator culture through adherence to exclusionary rituals within the academy. In contrast, hooks calls on critical theorists to embody their work beyond the page or the classroom.

Being the Change You Want to See in the World

Across all of her work, hooks provides an example of how to do embodied work. Reflecting the precepts of woman-of-color feminism, critical cultural studies, and other schools of thought that reject the positioning of the researcher as abstract, objective outsider, hooks shares her personal experiences and the voices of black women and men outside academia to theorize. In this way, she creates autoethnographic essays that viscerally illustrate the issues at stake and the ways in which the phenomena she theorizes about impact our lives in public and intimate ways. Indeed, I will note here that my first contact with bell hooks' work as a classroom assignment (I had read her work previously, but not as part of a formal course) was in a course on ethnography. We read *Teaching to Transgress*, as well as critical law and race scholar Patricia Williams' *Alchemy of Race and Rights*, as autoethnographic texts. We learned from these two black feminists how to interweave one's life stories and lessons with theory in ways that made the previously dull-sounding and hard-to-read post-modern and post-structuralist ideas in other works come alive. Reading hooks through the lens of autoethnography is useful, for it links her essays and criticisms to a methodology that is itself an outgrowth of the critiques brought by the intellectuals who founded Ethnic Studies, Women's

---

50. hooks, *Talking Back*, 33
51. Ibid., 34.

Studies, and Cultural Studies fields. She articulates how we theorize the world; we understand it and can make sense of it through our engagement with social phenomena. Through deep engagement with our life stories and the life stories of overlooked people, we illuminate connections that give insight beyond the individuals themselves and reveal a myriad of problems and conundrums to be pondered and solved. These alternative ways of seeing the world, from the bottom up, linking intimate experiences to society-wide issues, expand our imagination and make concrete the high stakes of theory.

So what at first glance might seem therapeutic or confessional is always grounded by the goal of facilitating critical consciousness and ideas for progressive change. To inspire radical shifts in our habits of mind to engender equality, freedom, happiness, hooks explores her own journey to critical consciousness as part of the work. As I quoted her earlier, it is not enough to name the problem—you have to provide visions of getting beyond the problem in order to give people reason to continue in social justice struggles. Moreover, the personal aspects of liberation are always to be incorporated into community life.

Many of the most effective passages in hooks' work showcase the importance of community to self-recovery. In contrast to the privatized (and corporate-sanctioned) versions of recovery promulgated in mainstream media, her accounts of self-recovery are fiercely political and spiritual in a very different way. Consider, for example, a recent *Oprah* magazine column by Martha Beck exhorting readers to take charge in their lives by redecorating their homes instead of just "complaining" like the feminists she met in grad school.

> Say you're wandering around your home, tripping over magazines you've been meaning to read, the clothing you've been meaning to donate. . . . [C]larify the change you'd like to see at home. Go into the least pleasant part of your living space. You may immediately experience Pushback as a desire to leave. Don't. Instead, figure out exactly what you can't stand about it. . . . Does that dark and dismal corner need a lamp?. .Imagine these things, letting the space suggest Possibilities. . . .
>
> To this day, some of the feminists I met in grad school are still complaining. They seem to enjoy it. I wish them all the best. For you, however, I wish something better: a new year full of clarity regarding the persistent problems in your life.[52]

Contrast this to hooks' descriptions of why she felt estranged in her New York City neighborhood, and how she found a sense of home, of clarity and belonging, in a small Appalachian town, not because of the right lamp, but because of the anti-racist community values there. When she lived in NYC's West Village, it became more integrated and gentrified by "The 'cool' white folks" who said

---

52. Beck, "Four Steps to Aha!," 38.

they wanted diversity, but in the end "their presence usually raised prices" and pushed people of color out or made them feel unwelcome, as hooks eventually did, experiencing coldness and disdain from her new white neighbors.[53] She no longer felt safe, part of the community. When she moved to Kentucky to be near her parents, however, she encountered white people who wanted to ensure that she felt welcome, that they understood that the community was invested in anti-racism and desegregation.[54] hooks found a home that pleased her because, unlike the hip, multicultural trappings of New York City, this Kentucky town contained people committed to, as Lerone Bennett Jr. said, the "reciprocity of emotion and relation between individuals sharing a common vision of the possibilities and potentialities" of humankind.[55] She found a place that had the potential for being a "beloved community" where her neighbors expressed an ethos of service, respect, and mutual partnership.[56]

Note that, in addition to trashing feminists as complainers, not do-ers, the *Oprah* columnist makes no reference to community, to the role of sexism in causing women's stress—who can afford home makeovers when the wage gap is still so wide?—or to any extra-individual element of life experiences. In contrast, hooks' feelings of self-recovery are deeply tied to her ability to feel at home, to feel free of racist surveillance or aggression. The conscious choice of her Kentucky community to be anti-racist, to change the town so that it doesn't continue its legacy of segregation in perpetuity, made her feel at home, even though it was a white majority town. As such, her essay on returning home to the South provides a strong example and evidence of change and agentic anti-racist action beyond the realm of complaints and cosmetics.

Agency

hooks' writings provide us with a range of examples of community and individual agency. She asks readers to recognize their choices and habits of mind as agentic. She does not, however, dismiss the fact that people are victimized and unfairly treated within dominator culture. Indeed, she takes writers such as Shelby Steele to task for mischaracterizing black victimization as a one-way street. Steele's *The Content of Our Character* argued that black people had embraced victimhood, a way of being that paralyzed them and distorted their vision of society, achievement, and identity.[57] He was joined by other famous black and white conservatives, such as Ward Connerly, who argued that the alleged "victim culture" meant Black people looked for handouts and took affirmative action-created positions without actually

---

53. hooks, *Belonging,* 76–77.
54. Ibid., 81.
55. Ibid., 85.
56. Ibid., 87.
57. Steele, *The Content of Our Character.*

meriting them.[58] But, while many folks—hooks included—agreed that embracing victimhood would be disempowering, hooks points out that

> his demand. . .was undermined by his insistence that racist aggression was no longer a threat to the well-being of black folks. . .[I]t was such an utterly unsubstantiated claim. . .Steele's will to deny this reality was linked to his refusal to call attention to the ways white Americans are responsible for perpetuating and maintaining white supremacy. By not calling attention to white accountability, he implied that black folks must assume full responsibility for the task of ending racism, of repudiating the victim identity. This seemed quite ironic given the reality that it was precisely the white repudiation of militant black resistance to racism that lay the groundwork for the emphasis on victimhood. . . . The image of black folks as victims had an accepted place in the consciousness of every white person; it was the image of black folks as equals, as self-determining that had no place.[59]

hooks insists that people need not be paralyzed by experiences of victimization, and do not need to "play the victim" when seeking justice. Rather, they need to acquire critical consciousness and join communities that support them in the process of resisting and challenging the forces that oppress them. But she does not want us to believe that rejecting a victim-centric identity will itself dismantle racism (or sexism); engaging in oppositional practices as well as fostering liberatory consciousness is necessary. It is also necessary for dominant groups—in this case, whites—to be accountable for their role in the racial system. Progressive change comes only when all are involved. Thus, whites AND Blacks must not only repudiate racism, but also the victim-centered identification of Blacks. "As long as white Americans are more willing to extend concern and care to black folks who have a 'victim-focused black identity,' a shift in paradigms will not take place."[60] If whites do not see blacks as agents who are capable of responding effectively to oppression, then they do not allow for their full humanity and imagine blacks as being always dependent, not equal. What Steele and others like him miss is the need to construct a relationship of equals, of mutuality, where blacks and whites can construct relationships not based on guilt, greed, or paternalism, but as co-creators of a new way of thinking. "Those white Americans. . .must be willing to surrender outmoded perceptions of black neediness that socialize them to feel comfortable with us only when they are in a superior, caretaking role" just as much as Blacks must reject a victim-based identity that lends them moral authority only when asserting victimization.[61]

---

58. See the insightful analysis of Ward Connerly's victim rhetoric in campaigns to dismantle affirmative action in Jones and Mukherjee, "From California to Michigan."

59. hooks, *Killing Rage*, 52–54.

60. Ibid., 58.

61. Ibid., 59.

Although acquiring the new ways of seeing provided by critical consciousness to assess one's situation is important, hooks is not saying that one's ability to
see the cracks in hegemonic cultural armor is sufficient to facilitate real, lasting
change. She is also not engaging in a celebration of psychic resistance wherein
individuals are "free" even in the direst circumstances. Rather, as Gunn and Cloud
countered, fixating on the power of an individual to choose "among differing
interpretations of reality" even when imprisonment or genocide is happening,
is the worst form of radical individualism and wish fulfillment.[62] Like hooks,
these authors remind us that agency is limited by context, and the "power" of
cultural critique is constrained by the resources and opportunities one has to put
theory into practice. Although a subject may exercise agency over the interpretation of her experiences of domination, her ability to change the sociopolitical
landscape—even to save her own life—is not merely a discursive matter. Instead,
hooks urges us to remember that freeing one's mind and embracing one's agency is
a necessary, but not sufficient, step in the process of liberation. One can be liber-
ated and practice critical resistance without having much power; one would still
be in danger of abuse from those who have more power and privilege.

Fostering resistance culture is necessary to ready oneself for the opportunities
that are bound to emerge to make change. As Cornel West remarked in a dialogue with hooks, when Rosa Parks was arrested in 1955, no one knew it would
be "the" catalytic moment of a new mass movement, but all of the oppositional
consciousness-raising and organizing activities that were well under way in Black
communities meant people were ready to engage in protest right away. So too for
today, when there is much frustration that more progress on racial inequalities has
not come to fruition: "we don't know what particular catalytic event will serve as
the take-off for it. . .but when it occurs we have got to be ready."[63] Building up
critical consciousness and community values is what makes us ready for transformative action.

---

62. Gunn and Cloud, "Agentic Orientation as Magical Voluntarism," 52.
63. hooks, *Breaking Bread*, 16.

three

Democracy, Civility, and bell hooks

I locate myself with. . . a wild crowd of known and unknown folks. We share a commitment to left politics. . . we are concerned with ending domination in all its forms; we are into reading and deeply concerned with aesthetics. . . [1]

How could participation in—or study of—this "wild crowd" contribute to Communication Studies theory? The previous chapter's overview of hooks' philosophy suggests certain applications to analysis of media texts, but what of overarching theoretical questions that have regularly occupied communication theorists? Being part of a culture of creative resistance makes one ready for protest, ready to join with allies. Having habits of mind learned from resistance culture and the support of a community are crucial. hooks declares in the opening pages of *Teaching Community* that we need "mass based political movements calling citizens of this nation to uphold democracy and the rights of everyone to be educated, and to work on behalf of ending domination in all its form."[2] Such a transformation requires us to name the problem and also "deeply articulat[e] what we do that works to address and resolve issues," so as to inspire continued struggle and progress, and to engender hope. Mass media and everyday communication practices are the means for articulating the problems and the solutions, representing, naming, addressing, and discussing how we make the world.[3] One way to

---

1. hooks, *Yearning,* 19.
2. hooks, *Teaching Community,* xiii.
3. Ibid.

illustrate how her approach invigorates Communication Studies is to put her into conversation with theorists of public discourse, civility, and democracy, such as Habermas, Dewey, and Mills.

This chapter provides an illustration of how hooks' work relates to other theorists' understandings and descriptions of contemporary problems involving democracy, communication, and inequality. In that section, I set her work in conversation with that of Jürgen Habermas, C. Wright Mills, and John Dewey. Like these men, she is a holistic scholar whose work transcends disciplinary boundaries to understand the limits of contemporary democracy. Habermas' comparisons of European nations' development of public spheres takes up multiple strands of historiography, sociology, and economics, alongside meditations on communication contexts and technologies, to make conclusions about the state of public discourse. Mills turns his attention to how intellectual energies are developed and focused, finding fault in the ways inquiry is conducted in many academic fields so as to dampen the "sociological imagination" that facilitates connection between individuals and democratic society, and the drawbacks of concentrating intellectual enterprise in the university. Dewey looks at the sweep of U.S. history and the impact of economic growth, education, social diversity, and technological change to understand the failings of our democracy to fully engage the strengths and energies of its citizens. hooks shares the concerns of these scholars. But hooks is more interested in exploring how relations of power structure our "habits of being"—including communicative interactions—from the mundane to the most spectacular, and finds dominator culture the root of the problem of limited democracy and social inequality.

Civility and Multiculturalism

Increasingly in her work, such as *Teaching Community*, *homeplace*, and *Salvation*, hooks passionately argues that we need to re-think and re-learn how to interact with each other, how to be civically minded. Here, I explore how her work illuminates this particular question of communication in the public sphere. It is particularly important at this moment in our history to think broadly and creatively about civility. We have seen in the wake of 9/11 the willingness of many politicians and citizens to brush aside concerns about civil liberties and respect for differences. Indeed, there have been loud calls to return to a model of assimilation to "get rid of" differences that seem toxic to "western" democracy. Since the election of Barack Obama, we have witnessed intense moments of political incivility, much of it expressed through demonization of gay and lesbian citizens, Black, Arab, and Muslim peoples, and undocumented immigrants. The culture wars, which ramped up as hooks began her academic career in the 1980s, have been revived, and many commentators are again laying the blame for America's political gridlock and economic stagnation at the feet of multiculturalism.

For example, the thesis of Daniel T. Rodgers' new book, *Age of Fracture,* is that since the mid-twentieth century the intellectual community has moved away from a kind of consensus around promoting sociality, the commons, and citizen contributions to the common good.[4] Starting in the 1960s, there was a shift towards fractured thinking, where the individual or subgroup became the most important units to think about, and as such we have lost our sense of common good or purpose, and with it an adequate analysis of how power works in our society. This is a lament that is much repeated in other domains, whether it be New Democrats who argue diversity scares away swing voters, or recent books penned by neo-conservatives who want us to give up on multiculturalism altogether, such as Dinesh D'Souza or Samuel Huntington.[5] Whether Right, Left, or Center, these critics are vexed by cultural, racial, gender, class, party, and other affinities, and wish we could just get back to finding a consensus based on some set of universal principles. The most Eurocentric commentators say we should trust in the Enlightenment of the West, and leave all others to burn in the fires of their own backwardness; others look to class as the defining common ground that will solve the "problem" of racial, ethnic, or gender difference. Still others hope for a sort of cosmopolitanism, where we learn to leverage and enjoy our differences in some egalitarian framework where no one is compelled to associate with any particular identity; others scoff at such a scheme as anarchic or utopic, and say we must just resign ourselves to intergroup tensions—it's human nature, after all, to prefer one's own group over others.

Regardless of position, most of the theorists, pundits, and everyday people who lament our seeming lack of common principles often agree on one thing: our public discourse is dangerously rancorous, so polarized, so ugly it makes us feel like we will never find any common ground.[6] We wonder if there is any room for compromise to craft policies that address pressing issues such as poverty, environmental destruction, migration, and gender equality, to name but a few. The media loom large here as a villain, oversimplifying here or ignoring evidence there, and encouraging bombast and vitriol to drive ratings ever upward. Where do we start, when everything seems destined to end in fractious bickering amongst endlessly subdivided groups? bell hooks offers us some ways to think about this conundrum that resonate with those of many communication scholars. The main difference for hooks is that, like fellow feminists and critical race theorists, the starting point is not necessarily the search for *consensus*, but rather the search for *equality*

---

4. Rodgers, *Age of Fracture.*
5. Modood, "Is Multiculturalism Dead?"; Roediger, "White Workers, New Democrats."
6. Herbst, *Rude Democracy.* I concur with Herbst that it isn't productive to ask whether or not American political discourse has become more rancorous, but rather to ask how civility is defined and deployed in political discussions.

amongst participants. To put it in the language of public sphere theory, she argues that our public sphere, norms of discourse, and intimate spheres have been structured by principles that promote domination of the self over Other. She uses the phrase "white supremacist patriarchy" to describe the dominator culture that is enmeshed in our institutions and that is reflected and reinforced by habits of mind and behaviors and the production and dissemination of cultural artifacts.[7]

To reiterate: hooks is not saying that only white men or white people are part of dominator culture, or that they will never be otherwise. Rather, hooks turns our attention to how a system of domination infiltrates all levels of society and relationships, making it inevitable that all of us will, in some way, have our perception tainted by it, or be rewarded for going along with the status quo, even if it means we hurt others intentionally or unintentionally. It means that we must resist and deconstruct the system of domination and recover from how the system has affected our own habits of living, thinking, relating to each other. For hooks, we can only have true civility when we put our shoulders to the wheel to dismantle the hierarchies of domination, and deconstruct how domination has patterned our habits of being. Once we unravel this tangled web, we can see and create ways of debating and discussing the common good that do not depend upon domination. Only through such a process can we open our minds enough to consider and imagine other modes of civic exchange.

This is an ambitious goal to be sure. But when compared to other theorists of the public sphere, the common good, norms of discourse, and the role of education and intellectuals in our democracy, hooks is in good company. She too provides us with big ideas for social progress that center on the transformation of human communication. hooks is clear that part of a critical theorist's job is to craft work that reveals the workings of domination within our everyday conversations and our most complex media texts. Reading hooks alongside the work of John Dewey, C. Wright Mills, Jürgen Habermas, and others, it is clear that she is contributing to a long tradition of philosophical explorations of how communication and intellectual development contribute to a good society, or, as Dewey wrote, the "Great Community." Her understanding of systems of domination and the role of the cultural critic can shed a different light on our current concerns about civility, and on the path she lays out for citizens to heal themselves and enrich democracy.

Like these other intellectuals, she works with ideal types, case studies, and sweeping historical and social narratives. Unlike many other thinkers who create normative theories, though, she moves between the big abstract ideas and problems to everyday interactions, often at a great speed that feels jarring to some readers, exhilarating to others. She talks about rage, love, memory, homeplaces, self-care, and psychological repair in the same breath that she describes the impact

---

7. hooks, *Talking Back*, 21–23.

of a law, slavery, a stereotype, genocide, and encourages us to re-tool children's literature. This makes her maddening to some, but accessible to many more. And I think she is so because she doesn't shy away from truly taking seriously the adage, the personal is political. That oft-misapplied tenet is a lodestar in her work, and imbues her writing with an immediacy and intimacy that is often at odds with traditional scholarly writing. And that, of course, is part of the point. We need different modes of communicating our ideas, with each other, across group boundaries, and within them, to create lasting change.

In the next part of this chapter, I outline how bell hooks' work injects important discussions of history, experiential knowledge, and the importance of creativity and dialogue to transform public discussions of crucial issues of resources and justice and, hopefully, inter-group relations. First, I delineate some of the overlap between Habermas' formulations of the public sphere and ideal speech situations on the one hand, and hooks' understanding of how communicative habits are shaped by dominator culture and resistance to domination on the other. Then I turn to John Dewey, whom hooks recognizes as an important thinker in education and social justice, a scholar who also conveyed broad, ambitious designs to educate citizens in order to create a more democratic society. Finally, I discuss how hooks' understanding of cultural criticism dovetails with C. Wright Mills' formulation of the sociological imagination.

Civility and Democratic Inclusion in the Public Sphere

Jürgen Habermas traces the origins of the public sphere to the private realm of the home, where families engaged in discussions of literature, discussions that eventually occurred in spaces outside the home (literary publics of salons and coffeehouses) and prefigured the critical discussions and debates of political issues by "private persons" who created a zone of publicity separate from the state, private, and market spheres.[8] Similarly, hooks emphasizes the impact of discursive training in the home, but she departs from Habermas' original formulation of private and public by recognizing the interpenetration of public and private via intersectional analysis of speech situations in the home. The patriarchal power imbalance and structuring of communication expectations impacted how one participated in private and public discussions, mirroring the dominant norms that devalued female speech. Like Nancy Fraser and other feminist critics of Habermas, hooks points out how the "training ground" of the private sphere did not allow for equal development of speech capacity. Similarly, in the public sphere, Blacks and women were the objects of debates over citizenship, deemed unfit to engage in "ratio-

---

8. Habermas, *The Structural Transformation of the Public Sphere*.

nal critical" debates and forcibly excluded from spheres of discursive influence.[9] And, while the gender dynamics of the private sphere worked in many cases to discourage female publicity, hooks explains how this training ground did nurture resistant thoughts and habits of mind on the lines of critical reflection and discussion of racial issues. "Watching television in the fifties and sixties, and listening to adult conversation, was one of the primary ways young black folks learned about race politics."[10] Thus, for African Americans, "private" spaces had to be used out of necessity to discuss "public" matters, because public spaces were not open to them. Kitchen tables and living rooms in Black homes were spaces where counter-public discourses and political strategies could be forged in relative safety.

hooks' work resonates with the idea (put forth by many critics of Habermas) that there are multiple publics that co-exist, supported by a variety of institutions and perhaps with access to different amounts of resources given the hierarchical structure of state and society.[11] Moreover, she points out that despite any bourgeois norms practiced in white public spheres, black people could not expect whites to operate within those norms if and when they tried to participate in interracial communication. Rather, white supremacy marked black speakers as inherently inferior and unwelcome in public speech. Black people were not meant to address white people unless compelled to by a white person, and then only to speak within the boundaries of acceptable utterances and with deference. This created a situation where black people often had to mask any counter-hegemonic thoughts or communicative behaviors for fear of retribution from white speakers. Even though legal apartheid was eventually dismantled in the 1960s, "the habits that uphold and maintain institutionalized white supremacy linger."[12] Because of these lingering habits and racial tensions, many black people still wonder whether, when they enter white majority spaces, they will encounter hostility, or mutual respect, from other speakers.[13]

As many other authors have noted, Habermas has addressed some aspects of these blind spots to power, gender, and multiple public spheres.[14] However, in general we can see overlap between his and hooks' understanding of the role of non-state and non-marketplace spaces to the development of critical thought and building capacity for public speech situations. And, notwithstanding the focus on bourgeois norms in his initial formulation of the public sphere, in some ways Habermas and hooks share the sensibility that the "ideal speech situation" is con-

---

9. For feminist and critical race-theory-oriented critiques of public-sphere theory, see: Fraser, "Rethinking the Public Sphere," In *Habermas and the Public Sphere*, ed., Calhoun; Pateman, *The Disorder of Women; The Black Public Sphere*, eds., The Black Public Sphere Collective; *Counterpublics and the State*, ed., Asen & Brower.
10. hooks, *Yearning*, 3.
11. Squires, "Re-thinking the Black Public Sphere."
12. hooks, *Black Looks*, 168.
13. hooks, *Belonging*, 86–87.
14. See, for example, Habermas' closing essay in Calhoun's collection, *Habermas and the Public Sphere*.

stituted only when all capable speakers are able to freely give their opinion without deception or coercion. Clearly, Habermas would not recognize the regime of a public sphere structured by white supremacist speech norms as anywhere near the ideal; his emphasis on inclusion and freedom from coercion flies in the face of the ways Black speakers were intimidated into deferential speech and/or silence. Dominator culture's encouragement of Black dissembling creates an always-already distorted speech situation. hooks' work is focused on how we might create different habits of mind and being that, first of all, make it clear that coercion and deception still structure many of our public and private speech situations. Second, she aims to encourage wider dissemination of theories and practices that provide means for transforming the communication dynamics of domination into practices that support dialogue, mutuality, and listening. And, although she is much more focused on resistance to hegemonic norms, hooks shares with Habermas and Dewey the ideal that citizens must build institutions and learn practices that facilitate their engagement in public dialogues about the common good. People need places, spaces, media, and educational resources that foster their communicative abilities and sense of mutual interest in order to engage in discussions about shared interests.

Domination and Communication Practices: Wherefore the Great Community?

Dewey's generative work, *The Public and Its Problems*, posits that the complexities and speed of modern life made it nearly impossible for our original structures of governance to produce real democracy. Real democracy is based in *community*, and as such democratic institutions must be rethought and revised in order to serve a society that is in flux, that has different challenges to meet never before anticipated by the Founders. As he wrote in 1927: "The Public seems to be lost; it is certainly bewildered. . .composed of rather amorphous groups."[15] Even though he credits the nation with absorbing "The stream of immigrants" from Europe with relatively little upheaval, "the consolidation has occurred so rapidly and ruthlessly that much of value has been lost which different peoples might have contributed. The creation of political unity has also promoted social and intellectual uniformity, a standardization favorable to mediocrity."[16] Thus, not only had the country grown and changed exponentially, but our communities were debilitated by processes of assimilation and displacement. A short digression here—I find it interesting that most people skate over Dewey's criticism of the rapid assimilation of ethnic groups. But as early as 1927 he made a similar argument to that which was made to the Supreme Court in defense of affirmative action in 2002's *Grutter v. Bollinger*: diversity brings intellectual vibrancy, new thought, academic excellence.

---

15. Dewey, *The Public and Its Problems*, 116, 122.
16. Dewey, 115.

This thesis, that the crisis in community is a result of rapid expansion and debilitated social and intellectual energies, is certainly a compelling one. It resonates with the themes Robert Putnam explores in *Bowling Alone*.[17] Decreases in associations and desires to have deeper ties to our fellow citizens continue to be key concerns for many researchers, and how to get seemingly polarized groups or individuals to participate in meaningful ways. Finding ways to interact civilly, to not be estranged, is important to sustaining democracy.

But hooks identifies the problem of our inability to grasp modern problems and interact effectively with our fellow citizens from a different perspective, telescoping out to look broadly at our social landscape and the origins of its many fissures. Not only were our original democratic structures of governance created on the assumption of small communities, but they were also created in terms that allowed particular groups to dominate over others. So, we must address the ways in which the underlying power structures affect people's ability to perceive and contend with social forces as they attempt to engage in public affairs. Moreover, while Dewey acknowledges that assimilation drains the polity of intellectual vibrancy, hooks is concerned with the ways that particular forms of knowledge and cultural expression—and social groups—are defined as un-American, deficient, and irrelevant to public affairs. Importantly, this includes concerns about how marginalized groups become the object of public discussion, whether it be via the media or in policy discourse. So where Dewey worries about the "amorphous groups" of the disjoint society, hooks worries about the ease with which certain groups are drawn in very clear terms via historically entrenched narratives of racism, sexism, and heteronormativity, and that the hegemonic framework for identifying and talking about these groups has specific, sometimes deadly, consequences.

So here the problem of democracy, communication, and groups is configured with power and identity at the center. For Dewey and Putnam, the main issue is how to coordinate and encourage community interactions such that people gain (or regain) a sense of the nation as a great community where individuals have a duty to engage in civic, civil discourse, to understand they have mutual interests and, eventually, to forge consensus about politics. hooks insists that if we want this kind of social coordination to succeed, our society first needs to confront and dismantle the nexus of power and identity that marginalizes certain individuals and groups such that they cannot even enter the conversation on equal footing. Racism, sexism, classism, and their related habits of mind and being must be transformed to create grounds for truly civil discourse. To have equality with our fellow neighbors and citizens, let alone be confident that our discussions will likely be civil, we have a ways to go to build trust, confidence, and willingness to risk being vulnerable.

---

17. Putnam, *Bowling Alone*.

So how do we create the Great Community and make our public discourse more civil? First, hooks instructs us, we cannot romanticize the past as a place where communities were stronger, more cohesive, and so forth, although there are lessons to be learned from the past. Whereas Putnam looks to rates of membership in civic organizations, hooks reflects on the quality of associations and reflects on the ways people are socialized to value or devalue community ties. She focuses in particular on how Black communities she was a part of took care of each other and passed down alternative habits of being in the face of oppression. But we cannot pretend that everything was well in the good old days, because the force of dominator culture warped even the most harmonious-seeming neighborhoods. Likewise, we cannot forget that our public discourse has always had a strong streak of incivility, which many public sphere theorists have noted. Here I would like to draw from Susan Herbst's recent book, *Rude Democracy*, to define civility as a vague, if important, concept that shifts in meaning across time and culture. And, though the past wasn't perfectly civil, our ancestors never had to deal with the 24-hour news cycle and cyberculture that amplifies incivility in ways unimaginable even in the twentieth century.

What is sticky about civility, even though its definitions vary, is that civility has social, behavioral, and emotional components. We value civility because we believe it will provide social glue, structure, and rules for us to cooperate and co-exist. We behave in ways that are expected in particular contexts to show that we support that goal of social cohesion. We feel violated, disrespected, ashamed, when someone acts uncivilly toward us, or we are caught out breaking the often-unstated rules. So, as Herbst summarizes, "some form of emotional self-control, as well as a sense of good feeling, is just as vital to civility in our day."[18] hooks has described, in excruciating detail, moments when her colleagues or audience members have trashed her or other scholars in public forums. She describes how she resists participating in the expected spectacle of debate as combat, fighting the impulse to dominate the other speaker, for this just deepens the problem. She instead tries to exhibit openness, to listen, to engage her verbal attacker in an exchange rather than meet the expectations of dominator culture. In a real sense, hooks allows herself to be vulnerable in mutual exchanges. She invokes the communal sensibility of her neighborhood where she "learned the self existed in relation, was dependent for its very being on the lives and experiences of everyone. . .the coming together of many 'Is'."[19] Listening to all the many I's is part of the "ethic of relational reciprocity, one that is anti-domination."[20] This does not mean that there is always an equality of outcomes or inputs: mutuality can occur even if people do not enter the dialogue with equal resources. Indeed, we don't

18. Herbst, *Rude Democracy*, 27.
19. hooks, *Talking Back*, 30–31.
20. hooks, *belonging*, 87.

have the luxury of such equality today, so folks of different statuses and so forth must commit to the ethic of reciprocity and be willing to be radically open to the ideas and experiences conveyed by the other I's in the conversation. Those who come together do so bound by a common yearning for justice, for equality, which provides space for community engagement.

Civility assumes a mutually dependent relationship, and does not have only a single goal: consensus. As Heinz Eulau wrote, "We have achieved the politics of civility when we are capable of asking not only, 'What is in it for me?' but also 'What can I do for you?'"[21] Herbst emphasizes Eulau's understanding of civility that "one of the most difficult aspects of civility and civil behavior is the ability to tolerate ambiguity. . .that clarity and consensus may not come" by the end of the discussion.[22] Now, in hooks' understanding of dominator culture, there is certainly a hierarchy imposed upon Eulau's two questions—dominator culture privileges "what's in it for me." When someone trashes another person for their ideas—or for just being who they are—with ruthlessness, without respect or care, we can see the traces of "what's in it for me" culture. In addition, dominator culture has little room for ambiguity, for listening to one another, for delaying decisions. Dominators want to win, whether through violent force, simplistic and brutal applications of majority rule, or manipulation.

Here we see the return to hooks' central concern: how domination operates at multiple levels—interpersonal, bureaucratic, intergroup—to shape our understandings of topics, controversies, evidence, and the like. Domination, based on whatever intersection of identities, fractures both the dominated and the dominant's sense of self, sense of position, and their ways of being. In the binary of dominant/dominated, relationships and identities are interdependent on the power differential. When a person who is a member of a historically dominant group is confronted with resistance from someone who is identifiable as a member of an oppressed group, conflict may ensue if the dominator-identified person cannot find a way to re-think her position, to see the Other in a new light, and continue the conversation in a new, open manner not dependent upon winning—that is, continuing to be in dominator status. In order to create a society of civility, in the terms set by Eulau and echoed in hooks' conception of beloved community and mutuality, we need to deconstruct dominator culture, and replace it with other viable alternatives.

So, for hooks, one of the most important duties of a critical theorist is to deconstruct the power/identity matrix, and to share and make new tools for such work within marginalized communities. In so doing, the critic participates in discovering and crafting new forms of association and knowledge production in solidarity with other people. As a cultural critic, this involves investigating multiple

---

21. Heinz Eulau quoted in Herbst, *Rude Democracy*, 28.
22. Herbst, 27.

sites where dominant ideologies are communicated and sustained. As a teacher, this involves providing students and citizens across a range of sites with tools and opportunities to reshape interpersonal communication as well as larger social debates. In both cases, it means fostering free thinking of a sort that empowers people to make connections between their lives, social processes, and political events.

The Role of a Cultural Critic in a World Structured by Domination

I am not the first person to associate bell hooks or black feminist thought with the work of C. Wright Mills. In particular, Mills' concept of the "sociological imagination" has been revived by thinkers such as hooks and Patricia Hill Collins, who suggested that a sociological imagination was part of intersectional thinking. For Mills, this particular form of thinking emerges from an individual's ability to locate himself or herself within historical context, and to see the links between history and biography. Developing that sensibility is crucial to making people see how they can move into public discussions of the good. The sociological imagination helps people "to use information and to develop reason in order to achieve lucid summations of what is going on in the world and of what may be happening within themselves."[23] Once people have the sociological imagination, they "experience a transvaluation of values: in a word, by their reflection and by their sensibility, they realize the cultural meaning of the social sciences,"[24] and more easily make the connection between "personal troubles" and "social issues."

Where hooks departs from Mills is in her recognition that people who have experienced domination often develop and foster a "sociological imagination" through their resistance to domination, not only through formal schooling. Indeed, schools may be sites of domination wherein marginalized individuals must create tactics to resist the devaluation of their culture. Whether constructing "homeplaces" where people can gather themselves and nurture their humanity and resistant readings of culture or events, or participating in consciousness-raising discussions, the sociological imagination can be, and has been, fostered outside academia. For example, in *Yearning,* she notes how as a child watching television, her family would talk about the black people featured, the way they were being "treated, [by the government] and the political implications of" their appearance.[25] Those lessons are vivid and legitimate elements of knowledge production, necessary steps in building the sociological imagination hailed by Mills. It is easy to see that it isn't a far stretch to theorize about the politics of representation, narrative, and hegemony, from such living-room chats.

---

23. Mills, *The Sociological Imagination*, 5.
24. Ibid., 8
25. hooks, *Yearning*, 3.

Just as importantly, the same social sciences that Mills wants the public to understand have devalued the experiential knowledge of oppressed peoples. Thus, for the public to understand the position and experiences of other groups, work must be done to validate experiential knowledge as part of the conversation. The cultural critic may do this in multiple ways. She can herself make efforts to show how lived experiences often dismissed as "private" matters, or "personal," illuminate and extend our discussions of social issues. She could demonstrate how social scientists have missed important details and significant variables when they dismiss or ignore the insights of wisdom formed within marginalized communities. Or she might point out, as Kang recently has with his overview of social and cognitive psychological research on racial attitudes, that in recent cases, social science has just now caught up to the insights of marginalized people.[26] This requires a cultural critic to move between spaces that have the power to validate knowledge and places that the academy has often viewed as incapable of producing knowledge. Moreover, it requires us to re-think where and how we transmit knowledge and seek to apply it outside of conventional academic spaces.

C. Wright Mills lamented that the changing artistic and intellectual landscape of his time would lead to the isolation of intellectuals in the university. He worried that the pressures from university presses and commercial publishers would have too much influence on what people studied and wrote. He viewed the public intellectual as "the moral conscience of his [sic] society," and did not want to see that conscience restricted to academic spaces.[27] hooks shares his concern; she has always positioned herself as a cultural critic for multiple audiences, and urges her academic colleagues—particularly those who label themselves critical scholars—to make their work accessible to wider publics to engender discussions and encourage people to make connections between their lived experiences and theory. She wants academics to make "commitments to seek to write theory that would speak directly to an inclusive audience," even if it runs against the conventions of academic culture.[28]

To put it simply, a critic is a kind of teacher, and teaching should strive to support interactive, empowering exchanges between people. Whether through written or oral work, theory, art, film, fiction, or children's books, the critic is charged with inviting the audience to join her on a reflective journey into a media text or analysis of a social problem. Part of that journey is to re-think one's own communicative practices, and to try on new "habits of being" that do not reinforce dominator culture. Also part of that journey is to connect one's own practices to the social relations of our time, the ways in which they are reflected in resistance and hierarchies. It's a tough journey hooks invites us to take. And some may ar-

---

26. Kang, "Trojan Horses of Race."
27. Mills, "On Knowledge and Power," 611.
28. hooks, *Teaching Community*, xi–xii.

gue she asks too much of us as individuals, as academics, as students, as citizens. But a cultural theorist is supposed to ask tough questions and to envision ideals to guide our actions. A philosopher deals in the big ideas, in thinking broadly, in reshaping standards.

Sometimes bell hooks is criticized for bringing a "New Age" vibe to these topics, interweaving stories of her Buddhist practices into her understandings of power and personal transformation, the act of listening and engaging in recipro-cal dialogue. These things seem insubstantial to her critics, and maybe they are, for those used to specific norms of communicating theory and analysis. But all of our intellectual traditions have cultural roots. The dualism of Western traditions is woven into the thought patterns of scholars trained in the U.S. and Europe. hooks was drawn to Buddhism in part because it resists the dualistic thinking that so many aspects of dominator culture employ to understand the world. Bud-dhism's both/and approach, the commitment to dialogue and achieving the abil-ity to be comfortable with ambiguity, to search for answers that are not either/or—these habits of mind are tools that can be used to provide alternatives to the patterns of behavior and thinking that support dominator culture.

Revisiting her work in the company of scholars who have been prominent in the field demonstrates, I hope, that her approach is not at odds with those that are prominent in Communication Studies. Rather, they open up enduring questions and shine light on key concepts in new ways, and suggest different paths for inves-tigating topics such as civility in the public sphere. Incorporating hooks' radical cultural criticism in our explorations is a both/and proposition, an invitation to better understand and engage questions of power and inequality while attending to questions of the public sphere, civility, and so forth.

To conclude, I submit that bell hooks challenges us to think of ourselves as communicators in a deep, profound sense. She lays out how power, media repre-sentation, public and private communicative practices weave together scripts for conveying ourselves and our identities, framing relationships, expectations, and assumptions. Race, gender, class, sexuality, and religion are part of this alchemy of domination, which sets up unequal relations that are repeated across a range of communicative practices. For hooks, the challenge is to recognize and relate how our current communication habits fit into the matrix of domination, and to facilitate the process of unlearning hegemonic ways of being that are reflected in cultural output and everyday interpersonal exchanges. Her call is perhaps even more urgent today as new media technology further blurs the lines between mass and interpersonal communication, and media producers have more opportuni-ties to reach us—and we to reach others—through multiple layers of the media ecosystem. Thus, while much of her focused critical work on media texts is par-ticular to the 1990s, hooks' overall theoretical framework and conceptualization of the relationships between media and society, media and individuals, media and politics, continues to spark questions and resonate with contemporary scholarship and public concerns. Her insistence on grounding her critical insights in standpoint theory, with attention to power and history, and her willingness to explore connections between individual and group experiences, have produced provocative, but fruitful, conjectures about media and culture. Likewise, her discussions of how social location shapes our ability to "see" or "not see" racism, sexism, or classism in the media, and her determination to illustrate how our choices implicate us in systems of power, provides models for scholars and students engaged in the study of communication and society.

ꝼour

Media, Power, and Intersections

Shaping consciousness via re-circulating domination—or opening space for contestation.

bell hooks approaches the question of media influence from the vantage point of critical cultural studies. Like Stuart Hall, she sees mainstream media as part of the hegemonic ideological system that has supported (and continues to reinforce) domination of people of color, women, and LGBT communities. She, like other theorists influenced by the Frankfurt School, notes that the mainstream media are still managed in large part by members of dominant groups and are guided by the drive for private profit. Schiller, Gandy, and other scholars of political economy caution us to refrain from underestimating how profit motives shape media industries and available representations of our society. This is not to articulate a simple conspiracy theory where a few evil apples decide whom to punish with discrimination, or whom to stereotype; anyone who works within, and benefits from, systems of domination can perpetuate the stereotypes and myths, and no producer or representation is "innocent" of the historical, political, and cultural context. Rather, this is the working of cultural hegemony within the capitalist media marketplace. hooks interrogates how the values and practices of the dominant culture are normalized in mainstream media, and thus reinforce relations of domination. Exploitative capitalist business models, embedded in a white supremacist patriarchal culture, have shaped representations of marginalized groups for centuries. Media representations are thus related to the legal and social structures that have oppressed people of color, women, gays and lesbians. Indeed, this is why hooks insists it is crucial for people to evaluate critically the recent rise in representations of people of color within a media system that has, for decades, either excluded or demonized non-white people.

bell hooks' meticulous analyses of representations of black men and women draw upon and take into consideration the history of representations of Blackness. Any individual contemporary film is always-already created in relation to its cinematic ancestry: the racial stereotypes and relational dynamics of pre-civil rights Hollywood cinema. These legacies of the past, moreover, are not just the product of individual creative work: they reflect the social and political expectations set by white supremacy. The Savage, the Buck, the Sapphire, and Mammy, and the other Black types Donald Bogle and others delineate in histories of race in Hollywood, reflected Jim Crow realities through visual, dramatic, and comic devices. These became normalized codes for including black people on screen. They were fantasies of Black "authenticity" that assured white filmmakers and audiences that Black people were in their rightful, inferior place. Thus, interactions with blackness in the intimate space of the darkened theater were "safe" and did not threaten racial hierarchy, let alone invite people to question the system.

Hollywood didn't imagine viewers seeking radical visions of Blackness—unless radical blacks were depicted as crazy or doomed to fail as part of the conclusion of the story, as in the tragic mulattoes whose bodies and demise reinforced anti-miscegenation laws and customs. Hollywood's reinforcement of racial hierarchy and segregation was woven into the infamous Production Code, as well as woven into labor practices where craftsmen and women of color were usually blocked from union membership and other job opportunities. This is the legacy of the U.S. film industry that contemporary artists and audiences inherit. We inherit a still-unequal world of fantasy production where proven formulas—action films, "star vehicles," "Chick Flicks," buddy comedies, British costume dramas—are deemed more salable to, and legible for, mass audiences. Other films that incorporate "new" groups or touch on themes rarely explored in mainstream film are often labeled "too risky" until self-funded risk-takers prove otherwise. As such, popular filmmaking has not had a very elastic imagination of Blackness.

But the dominant film industry is not all-powerful, and movies, TV, and other mainstream media are not simply narcotizing audiences. hooks draws from Stuart Hall to situate her complex understanding of how the mix of history, politics, culture, and personal pleasure, converge as media impact our sense of identity. That is, we do not (and media producers do not) come to a particular text with always-already intact identities. Identity, as Hall puts it, "is constituted 'not outside but within representation.'"[1] Media images and narratives, therefore, do

---

1. Stuart Hall quoted in hooks, *Reel to Real*, 274.

not provide a "second order mirror held up to reflect what already exists, but as that form of representation which is able to constitute us as new kinds of subjects and thereby enable us to discover who we are."[2] Therein lies the promise and pitfalls of mass media: these popular texts shape and reshape, challenge or confirm, our identities. Media can simultaneously open up or close down vistas for exploring ourselves and our communities.

For hooks, then, a central question is, in the moments of consumption, how do we identify—or disidentify—with the images, narratives, characters, and situations that purport to "reflect reality" or provide pleasure? How do representations of men and women of different races, classes, cultures, sexualities provide recognition of the self and others? What does it mean to recognize—or lack recognition—within the media system, a system whose visual and narrative vocabularies have been built on racist, classist, homophobic, and sexist foundations and assumptions? Her film criticism, as well as her discussions of popular music culture, interrogates the relationships between commercial media, audience pleasures, and domination.

bell hooks on Film

hooks emphasizes that films are cultural artifacts, connected to particular modes of production, commercial expectations, and rituals of professional and audience responses. They are produced within a particular political, cultural, and industrial context, which in part sets the boundaries of possible renderings of our world. Movies don't just appear: screenwriters concoct dialogue; casting agents narrow the list of eligible actors; executives gauge the possibilities of a film's success based on past box office returns for the genre or featured stars; and "greenlight" films they think will make a profit or burnish the studio's reputation in some other way. In the past, this process of choosing films to make was done in lockstep with racial segregation. No studios had African American or Latino or Asian executives calling the shots; those actors of color who "made it" in the movies were almost always relegated to subservient or tertiary stereotypical roles; craft unions blocked non-white members. Black directors who tried to work outside of the system, such as the Johnson brothers, were thwarted by Hollywood's lock on film distribution networks. Only Oscar Micheaux could claim any modicum of success before the civil rights revolution, and even he was unable to sustain his studio in the end. hooks would have us keep in mind both this history of structural exclusion *and* the representational regime that reinforced it. That most black actors were cast as servants wasn't just an artistic choice of a single bigoted director: That choice reaffirmed white supremacist logic that blacks were inferior and meant to serve whites. As Donald Bogle, Patricia Hill Collins, and others have detailed in their work, Hollywood created a set of black types, gendered imaginations of what

---

2. hooks, *Reel to Real*, 274.

"real" black people were like, early on, borrowed from minstrel shows and crystal-lized in blockbusters such as *The Birth of a Nation*. While many African American organizations protested the prolific use of the Sambo, the Buck, Mammy, and the Sapphire, the political and economic context—and near 100% white control of the film industry—meant that little changed until legal reforms were enacted.

But hooks reminds us that culture often changes at a glacial pace, and not without struggle. So while it was progress to see Hollywood begin to include more black people in its films in the wake of the civil rights movement, this increase in representation is not immune from the past. Having had decades of sanctioned, habitual, racial exclusion and stereotyping, what would it take for a new generation of filmmakers to break from the past? hooks answers this question through critical analysis of the surge of black representations in the 1980s and 1990s, some of which were authored by African Americans who broke into Hollywood. She does more than explore the representations made available in these films; she also uncovers the roots and reasons for the newfound interest in—and profitability of—Blackness at the tail end of the twentieth century. Her interrogation of critically acclaimed and/or popular-but-panned films is an accessible entry point for those looking for a way to understand critical cultural studies approaches to film, audiences, and power within the changing contours of hegemonic and resistant media practices.

Like other theorists of hegemony, hooks is interested in how power relations are normalized in cultural representations of "real life." Specifically for hooks, though, it is necessary to look not only at the normalization, but also at why those cultural products are *pleasurable,* even, at times, to those who might be negatively affected by the norms and values expressed therein. She is also keenly interested in how moments of inclusion of Others can continue to reinforce hegemonic under-standings of group relations and social roles. Investigating racial/ethnic inclusion in contemporary media is not just an exercise in comparing the number of actors or directors of color working today to how many made films in the past; this is too easy and blinds us to the practices and habits of dominator culture that may still affect or shape the emerging opportunities for members of previously excluded groups. Rather, we need to look at whether these moments of inclusion generate oppositional understandings of race, gender/sexuality, or class, and whether we're really seeing something new, and not just a recycled version of early film culture.

The Seductive "Reality" of the Movies

> Movies make magic. They change things. They take the real and make it into something else right in front of our eyes. . . . It may look like something familiar, but in actuality it is a different universe from the world of the real. That's what makes movies so compelling.[3]

---

3. Ibid., 1.

Part of the "magic" of the movies is that we have to suspend some of our mental faculties—willing suspension of disbelief—in order to "get into" a film. Of course this doesn't mean that we are zombies ready to believe whatever film directors want us to believe, but hooks reminds us that we must confront "the reality that most of us, no matter how sophisticated our strategies of critique and intervention, are usually seduced at least for part, if not all of the film, because at the very least the psychological processes of 'getting into a film' require" that suspension of disbelief.[4] Without that suspension, we'd never be able to experience the movies (or television) as pleasurable. And, because we have all been socialized, to different degrees, within dominator culture, the social dynamics and assumptions of that culture often seem "natural" when they are represented on screen. Most mainstream films reinforce socialization of dominant gender roles and racial expectations. This is done more subtly today in "multicultural films," where people of color share more screen time than ever before with whites. hooks calls on us to go beyond noting inclusion to scrutinize the means and messages of the new mix of identities on display. Inclusion alone does not upend dominant understandings of status, power, and political alliances.

Media, Society, and Psyche: hooks and Media "Effects"

I put "media effects" in quotations here to underscore that I am not suggesting that hooks belongs to the tradition associated with experimental and survey methods of gauging media impact on audiences. However, I would note that her work does resonate with many of the findings of media effects research (as I will discuss in Chapter Five), and that further attention to the importance of intersections has enriched the work of scholars in that tradition in recent years. Looking at hooks' explorations of media influence on how we see and think about ourselves and our world, we find a solid belief that cultural consumption does have lasting effects on our psyches, and that the media industry is instrumental in shaping consciousness, even as it denies any responsibility for the negative outcomes of that influence. Indeed, her discussions of media impact on our conscious and unconscious minds resonate with basic theories of socialization in psychology: we are influenced by our education, the stories we are told, the institutions we enter, our aesthetic experiences, and our interaction with available models of social roles and behavior, whether they be parents or media idols. Where hooks departs from conventional social psychological research is that she is not concerned with identifying what percentage of influence can be attributed to media. She steps aside from such positivist concerns to express her (far from idle) curiosity about how media representations support or undermine the culture of domination, and to what extent audiences have readily available opportunities to engage with media

---

4. Ibid., 4.

that defy status quo renderings of their social group, power dynamics, or inter-personal relationships.

Media provide tools and narratives that are enmeshed with one's life experiences in profound, if sometimes subtle, ways that often overlap or punctuate the lessons formally learned from parents, at school, or via other authoritative sources. Socialization and modeling are not additive processes, but integrated, subtle aspects of everyday life and learning. So for hooks, media are never simply tools that, in the right hands, will help us to defeat stereotyping or to forge the Great Community. The community and its individual constituents need to confront and engage one another, and sometimes a media text is a vehicle for engagement. But all too easily media can reinforce relations of domination, even when they provide pleasures to audience members. Thus, it is imperative to provide people with critical thinking tools and opportunities for discussion so that they can deconstruct and understand the ways media shape their consciousness not just in the moment of reception, but after the images fade from view.

hooks is interested in pushing her readers to explore how their most intimate moments might be influenced by media's contribution to their socialization, not just how they react to or read a particular television show or controversial film. Moreover, she recognizes that the deck is stacked to provide materials of a particular type to the broadest audiences. Mainstream media structures favor narratives that reinforce dominator culture, that reproduce stereotypes and obscure the experiences and histories of people of color, of women, of LGBT people. There are structural barriers to alternative content, and so we have to be aware of how the market factors into which fantasies and voices make their way into our private thoughts, whether through the silver screen or iPod headphones. When we consume media, we intermix public spectacles and private, intimate feelings and thoughts. hooks asks us to

> consider the perspective from which we look, vigilantly asking ourselves who do we identify with, whose image do we love. And if we, black people, have learned to love hateful images of ourselves, then what process of looking allows us to counter the seduction of images that threatens to dehumanize and colonize.[5]

The goal is not only to multiply opportunities for black people to make, or be in, the movies, but also to change how we see so we can view blackness with new eyes without replicating patterns of racial/sexual hierarchy. Placing media texts into a more complex context where the question isn't whether the representations are "bad" or "good," she is interested in determining how and why a particular text gets made, becomes popular, and how it is linked to or departs from the legacy of dominant imagery and narratives of the Other that artists inherit, like it or not.

---

5. hooks, *Black Looks: Race and Representation*, 6.

Media Industry and the Other

As I discussed earlier, mainstream media's record with communities of color is nothing to celebrate. hooks moves from the historical legacy of those racial/gendered representations to talk very insightfully about how contemporary enactments of multiculturalism don't do much to destabilize either the older regimes of representation or the current modes of dominator culture that define the limits of relationships between men and women of any color, interracial relationships, working and middle class, or homosexuality. She explores the subtleties and pitfalls of popular culture—as well as its pleasures and resistant possibilities—within a framework that rejects simple categorization of texts as positive or negative.

hooks acknowledges that any contemporary black media representation is always-already linked to the legacy of the visual, comedic, and dramatic conventions of past racial representations. She also notes that these representations were not only profitable for film or television studios; they also contributed to the psychological comfort of majority white audiences. The representations of "real" Black people as servants, punishable brutes, or lazy sidekicks reassured many white audience members that Black people's inferior status and the Jim Crow system were "normal" and "natural" ways for society to organize around racial difference. The stereotypes made the appearance of Blackness in the intimate psychological space of the darkened theater or the living room less threatening. Moviegoers weren't coming to see radical reconceptualizations of Blackness or race relations—unless such radical flights of fancy were punished, as in characterizations of "mulattoes" whose death guaranteed a return to the segregated racial order. The cinema, thus, seduced audiences with images of Black inferiority, segregation as an apt solution to the "race problem." And Hollywood profited from the circulation of these stereotypes and representations of unequal social relations.

Before declaring victory in the increases in representation of Black people in Hollywood, then, one must gauge how far from this legacy we have really come, and whether profits continue to be made from new, yet still warped, visions of Blackness. This requires attention to the quality of representations as well as: their relationship to the heritage of dominator culture, how audiences are invited to position themselves in the text, and the producer's desires. Such analysis necessitates that we acknowledge the polysemy of films and heterogeneity of audiences' responses, but that we continue to remember that audience power is "weak" in the sense that Hollywood producers have much more say in what films are made available, and resistant readings are insufficient to fomenting changes in content or decision-making power. These different layers of critical concern, then, help us understand why many debates over "positive" or "negative" portrayals in media can be distracting or unhelpful.

Most observers would agree that our past contains clearly "negative" representations of Blackness. The rapist "Gus" in *Birth of A Nation*, for example, is a particularly heinous fantasy character who justified the practice of lynching Black men on suspicion of sexual contact with white women. Beyond such obvious examples—many of which no longer circulate widely—it is difficult to take a litmus-test approach to media criticism. Limiting discussion to whether a text is positive or not misses the point in many ways and extends conversations that either have no constructive end point, or that reinforce a conservative logic of representation that doesn't challenge systems of representation and production. Say, for example, a film includes an African American female character who is an accomplished surgeon. This, the argument goes, is a "good" representation, in comparison to past movies that included African American women only as maids, which was considered "bad" and stereotypical. That more African American actors in general appear on screen in a wider variety of roles is "good," and past exclusion was "bad." However, for hooks, the issue of mere inclusion and status change in roles is not enough. First of all, upgrade in the social status of a Black character is not an unambiguous sign of "progress," from the perspective of intersectional analysis. There are still black maids working in the U.S. today, and there are far fewer Black doctors than Black service workers. Why is it "progress" for the latter's image to vanish from the screen? Why aren't there rich, robust portraits of working class black women available to audiences? What makes playing a maid "bad" and a doctor "good" if an increase in black doctors on screens blinds people to the fact that black communities are still grossly underserved in terms of health resources? In other words, we need to look beyond the commonsense, hegemonic framework that says being a professional is "better" than being a member of the working class and instead look to the context of the representations so that we can better compare them and gauge the "progress" therein.

Relatedly, if getting more people of color hired to play parts or direct films is "good," then if a Latino actor is hired to play a role that reinforces gender hierarchy, or homophobia, we have little room to move. If a homosexual director crafts a blockbuster film that reinforces patriarchal understandings of parenting, s/he will be a "success" in terms of market-oriented analyses and in the sense that s/he will challenge the stereotype that gay directors can't do well at the box office. We certainly want to combat that presumption, which is used in Hollywood to reject proposals or make different hiring decisions. But for hooks, if we depend too much on the simple equation of inclusion = good, exclusion = bad, some critics will hesitate to criticize movies or novels, or other cultural products, that include marginalized identity groups for fear that their criticism will decrease future opportunities for inclusion. In *Yearning*, she calls out some Black writers for their limited range of media criticism, and seeks to create "a climate where more black artists and intellectuals can do cultural criticism" that goes beyond the simple axes of positive/negative, inclusion/exclusion.[6] Accepting inclusion by any means is a "reformist" rather than a progressive interest, in hooks' view. If we acknowledge that media are "central to the construction of social identities," then the moment of inclusion cannot be the end of discussion of how media portray people who have been oppressed. If media influence our sense of self, of our group, and other groups, then quality and quantity are at issue. Again, the goal of media representation needs to be defined explicitly: If the goal is for there to be *equal opportunity to amass profits* from the media business, regardless of the political and social effects, then inclusion alone is sufficient. So, if that market-oriented definition of success is paramount, no one should complain if a black actor plays a maid, a thief, or a doctor: if s/he gets paid, it's all good. But if, like hooks, we want at least some larger share of media representations to contribute to a more just society, to foster our imagination of inclusivity and equality, then profitable inclusion without thought to content is insufficient.

hooks explores these themes in her critique of both schlocky and innovative films that have included people of color in major roles. In her review of Quentin Tarantino's *Pulp Fiction*, hooks conveys her admiration of this white director's construction of the film, its Rashomon-like rejection of linear storytelling, and the performances of the acting ensemble. At the same time, she resists the means by which Tarantino configures race and gender in his explorations of male bonding, violence, sex, and drugs. Although other critics seemed to buy his explanations for over-use of "nigger" and violence against women and people of color—and seemed more invested in Tarantino's "cool" aesthetic that recombined disturbing elements in a new way—hooks called the film out for its ultimately regressive messages about race and sex.

> Tarantino's films are the ultimate in sexy cover-ups of a very unsexy mind-fuck. They titillate with subversive possibility (scenes that are so fine you are just blown away—like that wonderful moment when Vincent and Mia do the twist in *Pulp Fiction*) but then everything kinda comes right back to normal. And that normal is finally a multicultural world with white supremacy intact. . .
>
> Tarantino shows us in his films that a good cynical read on life can be compelling, entertaining, satisfying—so much so that everyone will come back for more. But as the poet Amiri Baraka reminds us, "Cynicism is not revolutionary."[7]

hooks' critical eye zooms in on how Tarantino's white male characters "bonded" with black characters, but somehow the white men usually ended up on top, while black men died or were brutalized in excruciating fashion. Neither über-

6. hooks, *Yearning*, 5.
7. hooks, *Reel to Real*, 61, 64.

cool Samuel L. Jackson's character nor Ving Rhames' tough guy could win in the end—and everyone was still playing the same dominance game.

Two other box office draws, both of which starred Whitney Houston, the African American singer, recur in hooks' discussions of the limits of Black inclusion in Hollywood film: *Waiting to Exhale* and *The Bodyguard*. The former was an adaptation of Black author Terry McMillan's best-selling book of the same title about a group of Black women friends navigating family, sex, community, and work issues. The latter featured Houston as a famous singer in need of protection after death threats, protection that came in the form of a white male bodyguard played by Kevin Costner.

Under hooks' incisive gaze, *Waiting to Exhale* is exposed as a retrograde set of representations of Black men and women's relationships. Indeed, her major essay on the film is titled "Mock Feminism: *Waiting to Exhale*" because she was so shocked by the ways the film was presented as an "authentic" Black feminist text. In contrast to the publicity and hype, she found that the film's characterization of Black women reduced them to "'familiar' stereotypes [that] would guarantee the movie its crossover appeal."[8] The women were portrayed as gold-diggers and quick to anger; the men were ne'er-do-wells who were bound to hurt and disappoint their wives and lovers. What is even more insidious about this particular Hollywood concoction is that it trades on the notion of black authenticity in its marketing campaign and via the connection to—and endorsements from—Terry McMillan, the Black female author of the original novel. With *Exhale*, racial identity was woven into discussions of the film from the beginning. Though a white man wrote the screenplay, the studio publicity machine and interviews were deployed to underwrite the authentic blackness of the film, by pointing out that "Terry McMillan assisted with the writing. . . a great way to protect the film from the critique that its 'authentic blackness' was somehow undermined by white male interpretation."[9]

Although hooks dismisses the notion that McMillan's novel was itself feminist, she does locate in the book several strong elements and representations of Black community values and mutual support that did not make it into the movie script. She cites the subplot in the novel of the women engaged in a struggle to fight the predation of liquor stores in their neighborhood, as well as many moments of strength and tenderness between romantic pairs that were never on screen. It is no accident, she suggests, that these elements were sacrificed in order to amplify the stereotypical "recognizable" codes of blackness that populate the screen. That is, these codes were easily recognizable for white studio executives and audiences who are well-versed in the Black types Hollywood has manufactured for over a century, and that have sold tickets to theatergoers of all races.

8. Ibid., 69.
9. Ibid., 66.

That the film was celebrated as a breakthrough for Black people in the industry vexes hooks, and serves as an indicator of the shallowness of inclusion and the lack of critical responses to the film. She wonders why McMillan gave so many public endorsements for the film, asking: did she "forget she had written a far more emotionally complex and progressive vision of black female-male relationships in her novel," or was the payoff just too good to upset the apple cart?[10] The lesson of *Exhale* is that Black people can be involved in media productions that exploit "blackness as a commodity," and also that "the same old racist/sexist stereotypes can be appropriated and served up to the public in a new and more fashionable disguise" for profit.[11] Nothing created by or for Black people is inherently "Black" or progressive—and pressures to entice a cross-over audience make it even less likely that counter-hegemonic representations of Blackness will remain in the final cut. She chided other feminist and Black critics for not being more vocal about the film's regressive representations of Black people. She is particularly invested in the role of public criticism of *Exhale* and other Black-themed films because of how they are often "marketed as fictive ethnography, as in 'this is about black life,'" which further reinforces the idea that the films are a "window to the world" rather than a manufactured, particular, vision of Black life.[12]

In contrast, hooks views *The Bodyguard* as an example of a film that, while not marketed as a "black film," contains transgressive elements regarding race, gender, and class alongside dominant norms. Although the movie is conventional in many ways in terms of plot, she finds its representation of black women "far more radical than any image in [the acclaimed] *Crying Game*. The conventional Hollywood placement of black females in the role of servants is disrupted" because the rich Black singer (Rachel) has a white man (Frank) working for her as a bodyguard.[13] She is especially intrigued by the fact that the film portrays a Black woman's life as one worth saving, punctuating this exception with the question, "how many films do we see in the United States where black female life is deemed valuable, worth protecting?" Although the film ends with the separation of the interracial romantic pair of Frank and Rachel—a separation that "resolves the tensions of difference. . . by affirming the status quo"—hooks does not dismiss the film entirely, because of its moments of transgression that make a "meaningful intervention in the area of race and representation."[14]

The only silver lining to this cloudy mix of Hollywood images of Blackness is that, with the dramatic increase in and profitability of black images, we have more opportunities to strategically and publicly interrogate these images. We can

---

10. Ibid., 70, 73.
11. Ibid., 73.
12. Ibid., 5.
13. hooks, *Outlaw Culture*, 62.
14. Ibid., 62.

ask why these choices were made over others and hopefully begin to strip away the veneer of common sense, authenticity, and "naturalness" of film. hooks laments that this opportunity was not taken with the indie film *The Incredible Story of Two Girls in Love*. This film, which was lauded by many critics for its portrayal of an interracial lesbian relationship, contained both progressive and regressive elements. The "progress" of making a lesbian relationship glamorous was paired with the white female director's decision to cast a black woman as the most homophobic character in the story. Despite the fact that she said she based the homophobic character on her own mother—a white woman—she cast this hateful character as Black. hooks wonders why

> not a single reviewer asked her to discuss why she chose to cast this character as black. She could then have been asked whether or not such depictions perpetuate the notion that black women are more homophobic than white women. . . . Such interrogation does not take place because it is not seen as "cool." It's much more hip to engage in uncritical celebration of interracial same-sex desire.[15]

For hooks, aesthetic ethics require filmmakers and audiences to contemplate how, even within a narrative that privileges a marginalized identity, artistic choices may still be guided by prevailing stereotypes that mask themselves as "authentic" or "natural" ways to portray a particular type of person or group.

Meaningful interventions are harder to make, as mentioned earlier, when profit motives push media producers to consider the comfort of white audiences, imagined to be ignorant of, or hostile to, radical expressions of Black subjectivity. hooks notes that McMillan's text—which she wouldn't call feminist but in which she does find some redeeming representations of black humanity—was appropriated by white Hollywood in the same ways that some genres of rap and black/gay dance forms have been appropriated by dominant commercial culture figures and firms. Appropriation is a prevalent and problematic vehicle for cross-racial cultural production and contact, and hooks is adamant that we identify the political and economic motives of this practice and the resultant repertoire of representations and strategies that have emerged to shape specific modes of multicultural "integration" in the media.

The Problem of Appropriation

Appropriation is the process by which someone takes a cultural product of another group and uses it for her own profit or gain *without changing the asymmetrical relations of power between her group and the other group*. Appropriation is not a simple act of "borrowing" elements of a culture: this kind of borrowing occurs within

---

15. hooks, *Reel to Real*, 94.

a system where it is easier for one group to take from another without facing significant economic or political repercussions. The injustices caused by cultural appropriation are easily illustrated by calls for reparation and recognition of those artists whose work was never compensated by their imitators. Only recently, for example, have some white rock musicians who took words and musical notations from black blues musicians without paying for them—or even acknowledging where they came from—apologized for this exploitation and tried to compensate their blues heroes with recognition and revenue sharing. This example of music appropriation makes clear what was taken, what was lost, and why: White domination of, and privilege within, the music industry made it possible for white artists to take songs from black artists who had little legal or social standing to challenge them. However, there are more subtle types of appropriation in the realm of style, or the realm of desire to know about the Other, which bell hooks' work helps us delineate and explore. This is of particular importance in a so-called "multicultural" or "post-racial" age, where media encourage "mixing it up" with racial/ethnic/sexual Others at the same time that many deny race or gender or class inequalities still exist.

The problem of appropriation is featured regularly in the essays in *Black Looks* and *Outlaw Culture*. Crucial to hooks' theorizing about appropriation is recognizing that no act of cultural consumption or production occurs in a political vacuum. Rather, the systems of cultural production and consumption are inflected by race, gender, and class domination operating in our society. What is notable today, however, is how cross-cultural consumption has shifted from taboo to cool. Historicizing cultural appropriation reveals a new set of rules for an old game. Alongside colleagues in post-colonial studies, hooks suggests that many contemporary multicultural celebrations of difference still operate through the power relations established in the past. Specifically, colonial and apartheid relations set up an asymmetric relationship of cultural consumption, wherein white Westerners were able to experience "Otherness" via their domination over people of color, and viewed the differences between whites and Others as essential, unchangeable evidence that whites were superior/modern and Others were primitive. While some cultural consumption appropriated "primitiveness" to provide whites with a thrill, such interactions were largely looked down upon, or relegated to the margins.

Civil rights legislation not only opened up new legal vistas for the U.S. public, but also accelerated the "discovery" of "ethnic groups" that marketers could target and cross-market to white consumers. Whereas in the early part of the twentieth century mass marketers largely ignored black, Latino, and Asian American consumers and culture, commercial firms quickly got on board with selling and re-selling the Other and courting "new" ethnic consumers. But these expanded relations of commercial multi-culture did not erase the asymmetric relations of consumption, of looking, or profiting from an Other culture. Although it is an improvement that cultural cross-over is rarely sanctioned with violence or social ostracism, it may still function to exploit marginalized groups. Equal exchange is not guaranteed: the culture and/or bodies of people of color can be constituted in this new multicultural era as "an alternative playground where members of the dominating races, genders, and sexual practices affirm their power [through] intimate relations with the Other."[16]

The hyper-visibility—and profitability—of desire for Others is a break from the past, when such desires were taboo. On the other hand, these desires are usually framed within a consumptive context where history and power are ignored. That is, the desire to have an experience with Otherness—whether via music, movies, or personal contact—is not paired with, or understood through, a concomitant desire to change the status quo of race or sexual relations. Rather, the impulse to appropriate often emerges from a desire to change oneself, not society. When whites desire "cool" black styles, or dress like their favorite black hip-hop star, it is not necessarily a gesture of solidarity with black resistance to racism. Rather:

> The desire to make contact with those bodies deemed Other, with no apparent will to dominate, assuages the guilt of the past, even takes the form of a defiant gesture where one denies accountability and historical connection. More importantly, it establishes a contemporary narrative where the suffering imposed by structures of domination. . . is deflected by an emphasis on seduction and longing where the desire is. . . to become the Other.[17]

For the media analyst, then, the question becomes: When is cross-racial/cultural media consumption exploitative, and when is it questioning dominant norms to empower people who have been marginalized? hooks explores this issue in her analysis of pop singer/actress Madonna's abundant use of Black/LGBT dance and musical stylings in her music and videos.

One feature of cultural appropriation is the ease with which the appropriator erases context, history, and inserts herself as the master of a particular cultural domain. Rather than use the act of cultural exchange as a means to facilitate mutual dialogue and critical consciousness, Madonna reinscribes racial hierarchies by positioning herself as superior to the Black/gay dancers and singers who appear in her videos and movies. Although hooks grants that many of Madonna's earlier songs and videos were transgressive in challenging homophobia and violence against women, she finds her film *Truth or Dare*, the book *Sex*, and some of the related songs and videos, depart from that radical work. Rather than challenging and transforming dominant understandings of queer sexualities, these works appropriate and reposition what hooks sees as fairly traditional patriarchal sexploita-

16. hooks, *Black Looks: Race and Representation*, 23.
17. hooks, *Black Looks*, 25.

tion of women and LGBT people for titillation.[18] The representations of gay men and lesbians, for example, give straight viewers a chance to "see difference" but do not invite viewers to question their own heteronormative privilege as they do so. Likewise, Madonna's black and gay dancers are presented in *Truth or Dare* within a neo-patriarchal framework, where Madonna plays "mommy/boss" to Others who are, as she tells the camera, "emotional cripples." Although she benefits from associating with black and gay cultures, Madonna always positions herself outside of those cultures, which "enables her to colonize and appropriate black experience for her own opportunistic ends" and not ally herself with black political movements.[19]

hooks contrasts Madonna's appropriation of black and gay styles with films by Sandra Bernhard and John Waters, both of whom are white artists who drew upon black music and dance to make successful movies. Bernhard's *Without You I'm Nothing* shows the actress taking on the trappings of black women performers and music culture. But hooks reads the film not as a simple case of appropriation; rather, it is walking a "critical tightrope. On the one hand, it mocks white appropriation of black culture. . . even as the film works as spectacle largely because of the clever ways Bernhard 'uses' black culture and standard racial stereotypes."[20] Although hooks finds the film ambiguous in terms of where Bernhard ultimately stands in terms of racial and gender politics, the ambiguity and discomfort within the text makes it likely that the audience will think about the politics of representation and appropriation rather than take white appropriation as an apolitical privilege. Waters' *Hairspray*, a musical set in the 1960s, is more explicit in its politics. White characters in the film who choose to break the color line to dance with Black teens

> are in solidarity with Black people. When Traci says she wants to be black, blackness becomes a metaphor for freedom, and an end to boundaries. Blackness is vital not because it represents the "primitive" but because it invites engagement with a revolutionary ethos that dares to challenge and disrupt the status quo.[21]

In contrast to Madonna's use of black dancers as a foil to her superior abilities and celebrity, Waters' narrative makes it clear that black teens are equal to the white teens who join them on the dance floor in order to protest segregation. hooks provides other examples of egalitarian cultural borrowing in other essays, but the point is that one's race/gender identity are not sufficient to produce work that expresses egalitarian or transgressive perspective on race, gender, or class. This applies not only to white media makers, but also to popular forms of Black-oriented and -authored media located in mainstream and independent venues.

---

18. hooks, *Outlaw Culture*, 14–15.
19. hooks, *Black Looks*, 159.
20. Ibid., 38–39.
21. Ibid., 37.

Increased Black representations or access to media production does not assure progressive or radical content will result. hooks provides examples by analyzing popular forms of Black culture, such as hip hop, that have had mixed results, at best, in terms of debunking stereotypes and expressing radical understandings of race, class, and gender domination. Within the same song or film, transgressive and dominant ideas can co-exist; moreover, commodification of marginal group cultures can lead to reinforcement of domination. Her analysis of black masculinity and popular culture instructs us to avoid the pitfalls of essentializing marginal cultures as inherently progressive or anti-domination when we do media analysis.

Certainly there has been some progress in mainstream depictions in terms of black men, but hooks contends that "Negative stereotypes about the nature of black masculinity continue to overdetermine the identities black males are allowed to fashion for themselves."[22] She laments that alternative types of masculinity are in short supply in mainstream media for men of any color, and for black men, that limited range is constricted further by the raced and classed imagery that suggests black men are "savages unable to rise above their animal nature, a threat" to be contained by any means.[23] But in the realms of jazz music and sporting culture, she argues, there are different models for being a black man on display. Men such as Duke Ellington and B.B. King have performed in their fields and made statements to the world that resisted the brute stereotype. "Certainly the musical culture of blues and jazz had its roots in the black male quest for an avocation that would require creativity and lend meaning to one's labor."[24] So too in sports: trailblazers such as Muhammad Ali and Kareem Abdul-Jabbar leveraged their public profiles to critique racism, articulate Islam as a religion more open to racial equality, and prove they had brains as well as brawn.

However compelling these examples are, hooks reminds us that these men, "gifted and in some respects lucky individuals in entertainment and sports," are far outnumbered by working class men without access to those outlets and resources. Moreover, these compelling figures are also few in number compared to the constellation of contemporary Black celebrities whose profiles line up more closely with hegemonic masculine norms. The most accessible—and the most profitable—visions of Black masculinity that circulate in dominant media channels retrofit old stereotypes of hypersexual, dangerous black men for consumers looking for an exotic option. This is exemplified in popular music such as rap. hooks understands that part of hip-hop culture emerged from progressive Black and Latino youth who yearned for political voice to testify to the realities of suffering and oppression being ignored in mainstream media. Progressive rappers often articulate the need for intra- and interracial "ties that would promote recogni-

---

22. hooks, *We Real Cool*, xiii.
23. Ibid.
24. Ibid., 23.

tion of common commitments, and serve as a base for solidarity and coalition."[25] And, like other scholars of black popular culture and politics (e.g., Tricia Rose, Melissa Harris-Lacewell, Robin Kelley, and others), she is simultaneously troubled by the ways the progressive potential of this form has been muted in mainstream media. She reads the shift away from politically focused hip hop to wildly profitable gangsta rap as a particularly troubling example of how a resistant form of black/Latina/o youth culture was transformed into a variation on dominator culture via commodity capitalism's newfound desire to market difference. hooks asks why gangsta rap, popular novels, and films seem to focus so much attention on the so-called "black underclass" or "ghetto" life, even when authored by folks who are not from the ghetto.

> The point of raising this question is not to censor but rather to urge critical thought about a cultural marketplace wherein blackness is commodified in such a way that fictive accounts of black underclass life, in whatever setting, may be more lauded, more marketable than other visions because mainstream, conservative white audiences desire these images. As rapper Dr. Dre calls it: "People in the suburbs, they can't *go* to the ghetto so they like to hear about what's going on. Everybody wants to be down."[26]

But being "down" with these visions often results in continued dehumanization of the actual black underclass, and no connection is made between "mainstream hedonistic consumerism and the reproduction of a social system that perpetuates and maintains an underclass."[27]

Of course, she calls rappers and their fans to take responsibility for hyping macho, violent, misogynist fantasies as "keeping it real." But she is also clear that the emergence and popularity of gangsta is not simply a peculiar artifact of Black culture; rather, this music culture has origins not only in an "authentic black experience," but also in the values of dominator culture. Moreover, gangsta rap has been promoted aggressively by white-dominated multinational corporations and is eagerly consumed by white listeners (as well as fans of every color and creed) because it resonates with already-existing understandings of masculinity, class, and race.

> More than anything, gangsta rap celebrates the world of the material, the dog-eat-dog world. . . Significantly, the logic [of gangsta] is a crude expression of the logic of white supremacist capitalist patriarchy. . . "individual (cowboys), material (gangsters), and philistine." This general description of mainstream culture would not lead us to place gangsta rap at the margins of what this nation is about but the center. . . an embodiment of the norm.[28]

---

25. hooks, *Yearning*, 27.
26. hooks, *Killing Rage, Ending Racism*, 181.
27. Ibid., 182.
28. hooks, *Outlaw Culture*, 117.

Rather than seeing rap as a purely "black thing," then, hooks reveals again the ways that racial essentialism obscure intersections of power and identity in the marketplace. Her observations dovetail with those of Paul Gilroy, who, in *Against Race,* challenged those scholars who view black cultural output as emanating from a single wellspring of Afrocentric liberatory traditions that can be traced to the origins of music, literature, and other aesthetic modes. What this origin narrative of authentic blackness overlooks is how class, gender, and sexual differences up-end the essentialist claims often made that are based on origin stories.

> Class divisions inside black communities have been highlighted by the emer-
> gence of postmodern consumer culture. However, rather than accept the eco-
> nomic and social logic of this historic change, ethnic absolutism has joined with
> nostalgic nationalisms and argued that "race" remains the primary mode of divi-
> sion in all contemporary circumstances. . . . [But] corporate traffickers in black
> culture have become right from ensuring that [black cultural products] are no
> longer only the natives' dreams.[29]

Thus, many rappers called on fans to memorialize dead rapper Eazy-E not as a "griot" in the tradition of Afrocentric storytelling often associated with rap's origins, but as an entrepreneur who *chose* to be a gangsta in order to get paid and gain class mobility.[30] There is nothing "natural" or particularly "black" about the desire to make money.

If our analytical framework does not account for the intersections of race, class, and gender, our understanding of cultural phenomena will be shallow. In-tersectional analysis of media broadens our understanding of the place and role of Black men and women in the cultural imaginary as well as the industry. Moreover, this vision suggests a specific set of remedies: creation of cultural and intimate spaces where Black men and women can re-imagine femininity, masculinity, and other identity constructs that currently box them in to limited ways of being hu-man. Hooks notes that this is not impossible within the current regime of media and race relations: a good number of Black men and women now have access to media production and financing, and she criticizes them for not using those resources to promote resistance to dominant media renderings of Black men and women.

> I have often pondered why no body of resistance literature has emerged from
> black males even though they actually own magazines and publishing houses.
> They have control over mass media, however relative. The failure lies with the
> lack of collective radicalization on the part of black men (most powerful black
> men in media are conservatives who support patriarchal thinking).[31]

---

29. Gilroy, *Against Race,* 254–55.
30. Ibid., 264–66.
31. hooks, *We Real Cool,* xvii.

This pessimistic assessment of profitable black-owned media spaces, however, does not mean all is lost; hooks is still adamant that media provide productive sites of resistance. The question is how to get a critical mass of alternative media and politically aware audiences involved.

The Importance of Independent Production

hooks is one of many scholars and activists who argue that it is important symbolically and communally to have members of marginalized groups explore and create culture themselves. This argument is not about who has the "right" to represent "us" in a "positive" or "negative" light, because it's too easy to put the kibosh on that argument as censorship or restricting artistic license. Rather, this is about self-empowerment, self-realization, and creating means for a people to produce and engage with different visions of identity, practice new ways of seeing, and gain a broader sense of the possibilities of getting it done.

Dominator culture positions people of color as objects rather than subjects. Thus, one part of creating independent media for marginalized racial groups is to gain greater agency and perform subjectivity.

> Moving from silence to speech is for the oppressed, the colonized, the exploited, and those who stand and struggle side by side a gesture of defiance that heals, that makes new life and new growth possible. . . . No mere gesture of empty words, that is the expression of our movement from object to subject—the liberated voice.[32]

This transition is crucial. Being an object means being someone who neither perceives nor understands her world—she must be told what to do, what to think, whom to be. Objects are told when and where to look, how to frame their view. Quite literally, hooks reminds us, enslaved African Americans and black people living under Jim Crow were punished for looking directly at white people—particularly in the case of Black men looking at white women. They were punished for speaking about racial inequality or for confronting it with their gaze, their art, or their words.[33] Thus, there is a radical element in the idea of a black independent cinema that provides ways of seeing the world that disrupt or challenge the conventions created in white-dominated Hollywood films. While not guaranteed, black independent filmmaking creates space for black subjects to reject their objectification, to move from object to subject and provide new ways to imagine our humanity. hooks traces this movement in the works of Charles Burnett, Julie Dash, and other black filmmakers who use film to reframe blackness and sexual-

32. hooks, *Talking Back*, 9.
33. hooks, *Killing Rage*, 35–36.

ity, labor and bodies, for audiences who are often disoriented when they first interact with these alternative visions of African American lives.

We need to appreciate and support the ability of marginalized communities to dream up alternative aesthetics and worldviews that counter the dominant depictions of their experiences in mainstream media. She cites directors such as Dash, Burnett, and Marlon Riggs as strong examples of image-makers who have provided audiences with opportunities to see Black people—men and women—in a profoundly different way. They didn't just substitute black characters into the usual Hollywood stories; these filmmakers committed to reimagining blackness on screen.

> [Independent Black filmmakers] do not simply offer diverse representations, they imagine new transgressive possibilities for the formulation of identity. . . . Cinematically, they provide new points of recognition, embodying Stuart Hall's vision of a critical practice that acknowledges that identity is constituted "not outside but within representation" and invites us to see film "not as a second-order mirror held up to reflect what already exits, but as that form of representation which is able to constitute us as new kinds of subjects and thereby enable us to discover who we are."[34]

In an interview with Julie Dash, hooks remarked how her film *Daughters of the Dust* was a challenge for many critics and viewers because Dash had created a very different image of the Black past, Black culture, and Black family life. The filmmaker was aware that most people going to advance screenings would not have any prior contact with the cultural references she drew upon for the film, and so she "provided a press kit that . . . included character descriptions and symbols and everything that's in the film in order to acquaint the uninitiated."[35] hooks replied that the film requires people to

> interrogate the Eurocentric biases that have informed our understanding of the African American experience. I mean, we've never been taught, most of us, in any history class that black people had different languages, had different religious practices, etc. . . . [T]he challenge is to see blackness in a new way.[36]

To make the point more clearly, hooks compares the experience of going to an independent black film to seeing a foreign language film. Like John Berger, Laura Mulvey, Ella Shohat, and Robert Stam, and other scholars, who have unraveled how we are taught to see the world from particular gendered/national/raced standpoints, hooks is concerned that our visual vocabulary is determined, in large part, by conventions that are rooted in dominator culture. Most Hollywood films,

34. hooks, *Reel to Real*, 274.
35. Dash, *Daughters of the Dust*, 39.
36. Ibid.

even today, privilege the vantage point and experiences of white male subjects. We are invited into the film to feel pleasure through the vantage point of their experiences, their ability to control their world, usually through domination. We are rarely invited to take pleasure in resistance, in mutuality, in freedom. Those conventions are affirmed as "realistic" or "relatable" depictions (and profitable ones) and are hard to shake within the confines of the risk-averse Hollywood studios. Thus, independent production is necessary for experimentation, experiments that may, eventually, be incorporated into more conservative media venues. This "cross-over" between the indie and Hollywood film worlds is quite visible in spaces such as the Sundance Film Festival, and has also been part of the ethnic film festival circuit.[37] The slow, often sporadic entry of Black filmmakers into Hollywood raises questions similar to those raised by the popularity of gangsta rap artists: what responsibility do Black artists have—if any—when creating media?

hooks does not believe that Black filmmakers are born knowing they have a special duty to the black community. Rather, she wants us to acknowledge that our film and television industries have been shaped by white supremacist patriarchal aesthetics: the conventions of film have been forged by people who were themselves products of this dominant culture. From the predominance of the male gaze as the grounding perspective, to the casting that glamorized white women above all other women, the images of Hollywood valued whiteness and relegated people of color to the periphery. Given this history, hooks argues that we must talk about the "ethical dimension to aesthetic choices" that is rarely talked about since we like to pretend that "images are politically neutral."[38] The normalization of, say, the black comic sidekick, the kid from the ghetto, or the sassy black maid/secretary, is unremarked upon by most people watching contemporary films, especially when the notion of "inclusion" is considered the primary goal. As long as there are diverse faces on screen, then we shouldn't complain unless there is some blatantly racist portrayal or act. And, because these images are packaged in a pleasurable fashion, images that counter the status quo may cause discomfort in audiences who have become accustomed to the narrow range of characterizations of people of color, women, or gay and lesbian figures. "Hegemony requires that ideological assertions become self-evident cultural assumptions. Its effectiveness depends on subordinated peoples accepting the dominant ideology as 'normal reality or common sense.'"[39]

If we think in terms of aesthetic ethics, then Black people are not the only people responsible for writing, directing, or acting in a film that is progressive in terms of racial representations. Indeed, hooks credits white filmmaker John Sayles, and others, for challenging some pernicious aspects of white supremacist

---

37. Squires, *African Americans and the Media*.
38. hooks, *Reel to Real*, 90–91.
39. Ibid., 93.

film culture. Part of hooks' critique of an essentialist approach to thinking about responsibility for images is to promote awareness that it isn't racial identity that ensures radical or subversive content in media; it's "the perspective of the film-maker" as well as the economic forces that determine the resources available to her. Moreover, she is concerned that, especially now that there is a more profitable "market" for black images in Hollywood, it remains difficult (for new reasons) to create radical imaginings of blackness on the silver screen. Of course, independent filmmakers (black or otherwise) continue to face uphill battles when they propose films that don't line up easily with already existing genre conventions or cast ready-made stars. And, as more black directors and writers become insiders, will they bring in perspectives that challenge and comment on the legacy of oppressive stereotypes, or will they mine that legacy, updating it alongside their white counterparts to make money off new jack comedy and violence? Instead of offering a new aesthetic, hooks sees too many black filmmakers using their access to "address the huge white movie going audience by providing them with familiar images of blackness. These images are usually stereotypical."[40]

Filmmakers who go against the prevailing grain usually lack the same resources and backing available in Hollywood, and they have another challenge: how to convince audiences that it is worth their time (and money) to see a film that might challenge their habits of seeing. As I will discuss in the next chapter, hooks is emphatic that Black artists and critics work with communities to foster openness to seeing films in a new way, and to wrestle with any initial discomfort with "foreign" representations of womanhood, blackness, or gayness so they can see differently inside and outside of the screen. "Until both colonizer and colonized decolonize their minds, audiences in white supremacist cultures will have difficulty 'seeing' and understanding images of blackness that do not conform to the stereotype."[41]

For hooks, then, consuming the work of independent filmmakers such as Dash, or Essex Hemphill, is part of a process of self-healing, of recuperating one's sense of self and place in the world by confronting the reality that there exists a "cycle of damage that must be broken" in order to make us "free and whole."[42] Having alternative aesthetics that enrich our ability to imagine other ways of being a man, a woman, a black person, is crucial to resisting the "common sense" of hegemonic logics of domination. As Dash put it,

> I'm always asking people, when was the last time you saw a film about a black woman who is a trapeze artist. . . [or] on a rocket ship to the moon. It's like "What?" and then not have it be something about race or being raped or being

---

40. Ibid., 90.
41. Ibid.
42. hooks, *We Real Cool*, 143.

addicted. . . . Forget about black women having a zest for life, a productive life, successful. . . . That's too much.[43]

Independent filmmakers who dare to show the trapeze artist are often ma-ligned for not being "realistic" about black life. But hooks recalls again and again that cinema is not about "real" life; it is not an anthropological dissection of Afri-can American existence. Film is about fantasies, and we can reconsider our selves when immersed in a fantasy world that isn't structured only by racial and gender domination.

hooks argues that given the patriarchal orientation of our culture, this is per-haps harder for men because they have not had an equivalent set of tools as femi-nists to rethink gender roles. She urges Black men to let go of the idea that all they need to do is be "better patriarchs" to advance black freedom, and sees the work of black feminist and homosexual filmmakers as facilitators of that dreaming. This is not about a rigid "role model" framework of media effects—this is simul-taneously more subtle and profound for hooks. She acknowledges that exposure alone is insufficient to remaking one's worldview, but she accepts—and testifies to—the power of exposure to art as a powerful influence, a window to other ways of being, something that can strike one's soul in a way that no litany of political argument can.

hooks is committed to making it clear that we have options as readers, watch-ers, creators of media. She reaches into the archives of her own experiences with aesthetic pleasures that are not connected to dominator culture, where nurturance and mutual regard are depicted as pleasurable and rewarding. In childhood, for example, she shares how she appreciated how her female relatives created beautiful settings within their homes, encouraging her to think about, and feel deserving of, beautiful surroundings. "Art was necessary to bring delight, pleasure, and beauty into lives that were hard, that were materially deprived. It mediated the harsh conditions of poverty and servitude. Art was also a way to escape one's plight."[44] But hooks is not merely talking about daydreaming; she is describing conditions within which one can resist the dehumanizing effects of racism and sexism, if only for the precious moments of being at home rather than in the workplace, in school, or on the streets, where one's psyche can be overwhelmed by hegemonic ideologies and expected behaviors. Pleasurable aesthetics can provide space for the imagination to go beyond the daily conditions of oppression, to re-think one-self as worthy of beauty, as being capable of more than the roles proscribed by dominant forces. We often compare or measure ourselves against representations, art, artifacts, narratives, tales, and as such we consciously and unconsciously in-corporate the aesthetics of our environment—whether generated by quilt makers

---

43. Dash, *Daughters of the Dust*, 42.
44. hooks, *Yearning*, 105–106.

or television producers—as we navigate our lives. Thus, attending to how people understand and experience pleasures, gauge aesthetics, and engage in criticism of the popular arts of our culture, is important work, and is connected intimately to questions of power and resistance.

But hooks is also cautious to frame the "power" of critical reading specifically as it relates to other sociopolitical realities. Like Stuart Hall and other critical theorists, resistant spectatorship should be a beginning, not an end, to engagement with hegemonic ideologies and structural inequalities. Moreover, our realization that dominant media texts encourage or normalize harmful and dehumanizing ways of being should spur us to engage in critique and to seek alternative cultural sustenance. "Opposition is not enough. In that vacant space after one has resisted there is still the necessity to become—to make oneself anew."[45] So, if audience members who engage in critical spectatorship do not go beyond their armchair resistance, hooks sees few opportunities to foment lasting change in terms of our society and its cultural influences. Even if individual audience members impose a progressive interpretation on a regressive film, "this act of mediation does not change the terms of the film."[46] Supporting independent media artists, pursuing opportunities to protest regressive representations, and engaging others in media literacy are necessary elements of changing media culture and advancing progressive politics. Because domination infiltrates our most intimate moments—our psyches and souls—we must be prepared to struggle with ourselves and re-build our intimate spaces as well as our public spaces. They are not separate, binary entities, but interrelated.

Why Intersectional Analysis Is Critical to Changing Media and Audience Sensibilities
"A film may have incredibly revolutionary standpoints merged with conservative ones. This mingling of standpoints is often what makes it hard for audiences to critically 'read' the film's overall narrative."[47] hooks cites the example of the film *Sankofa*, an independent Black film heralded for its innovative portrayal of Black diasporic people, but yet still framed within patriarchal norms. This is not to say that hooks is desperately seeking the perfect film with all facets of identity done "correctly." Rather, intersectional analysis requires us to continue exploring the ramifications of, and interventions made by, films beyond a single category of identity. Tracking the interaction between race/gender/class/sexuality is part of the critic's job for any and every film.

Take, for example, her evaluation of Jane Campion's *The Piano*. The central character is a white woman negotiating a new life in colonial New Zealand, and many critics considered the film a feminist triumph. But hooks illuminates

---

45. Ibid., 15.
46. hooks, *Reel to Real*, 4.
47. Ibid., 3.

how the main character's story and the consequences of her attempts to conduct an affair situate her squarely within conventional patriarchal norms for woman's place. hooks questions why the highbrow cinematic trappings of *The Piano* seem to make it immune from the kind of criticism of misogyny that is abundant in discussions of rap music. The film features terrifying scenes of a white husband who sexually assaults his wife, then later, enraged, terrorizes her and his step-daughter by chopping off the wife's finger with an axe. Despite this, "Reviewers and audiences alike seem to assume that Campion's gender, as well as her breaking of traditional boundaries that inhibit the advancement of women in film, indicate that her work expresses a feminist standpoint."[48] This essentializing move—that a white female director is unquestionably going to produce a feminist film—erases what hooks sees as the quite retrograde representation of female "freedom" in the film—freedom the main character gains through marriage to a different man rather than in finding a way to develop and maintain her passion for music and sustain her daughter.

Many scholars in media studies have used intersectional analysis, and cite hooks' criticism as inspiration, or for theoretical guidance. Ronald Jackson III's *Scripting the Black Masculine Body*, for example, rigorously employs intersectional analysis to delineate the myriad ways that Black men are represented and signified upon in American popular culture and political reckoning.[49] Ralina Joseph's articles on media treatment of First Lady Michelle Obama and celebrity model Tyra Banks employ Black feminist theory's intersectional approach to identities and power to delineate how famous black women negotiate, oppose, and, at times, appropriate, norms of femininity and class in order to talk back.[50] There are many more examples in Communication and Media Studies, but what is important to note about these works is how each goes beyond simple positive/negative pronouncements to illuminate the nuanced identity politics that are contained within media texts.

hooks' work, and the research of scholars who adopt her approach, pushes the conversation towards more complex understandings of the ways in which hegemonic ideologies adapt to and are challenged by the increasing presence—and demand for—people of color in the media. They also help us to understand how and why seemingly "old-school" stereotypes continue to recur in contemporary media imaginings of class, race, gender, and sexuality. The goal of these works, though, should not be just to illustrate the dynamics for an academic audience; an essential next step, for hooks and many of the authors cited here, is to translate academic findings to share with lay audiences. This effort is part of the consciousness-raising "decolonizing the mind" that hooks believes is necessary to transform

---

48. hooks, *Outlaw Culture*, 120.
49. Jackson III, *Scripting the Black Masculine Body*.
50. Joseph, "*Hope* Is Finally *Making a Comeback*"; Joseph, "'Tyra Banks Is Fat': Reading (Post-) Racism."

society. The next chapter explores hooks' understanding of audience-media inter-actions, beginning with her approach to rethinking how audiences are imagined and formed—both by the media industry and in communities—and then turn-ing to the contours and limitations of audience interpretations of media texts.

⸾five⸝

Reception, Resistance, and Recovery

Many times people will say to me that I seem to be suggesting that it is enough for individuals to change how they think. . . . It has a patronizing sound, one that does not convey any heartfelt understanding of how a change in attitude (though not a completion of any transformational process) can be significant for colonized/oppressed people.[1]

This chapter links the terms reception, resistance, and recovery precisely because all three are integral to hooks' understanding of why popular media culture is important to study in relation to struggles against domination. Unlike many audience researchers, hooks does not end her inquiry after categorizing and comparing audience reactions to texts, or matching up their interpretations of meaning with prevailing or countervailing wisdom. Rather, she considers critical spectatorship, discussion, and reflection part of long-term processes of recovery that are necessary to heal communities ravaged by the inequities and indignities of racism, classism, sexism, and homophobia. Returning to the adage "the personal is political," hooks' framework for audience study demands that we figure out not only *how* people are reading texts, but also *whether* their readings and discussions can foster the kind of oppositional consciousness needed to re-imagine one's identity and destiny in the world.

---

1. hooks, *Teaching to Transgress*, 47.

The first part of this chapter outlines how hooks' work in black feminist thought and film criticism has influenced, and resonates with, key works in qualitative and quantitative audience studies. This section will synthesize her commentaries about audiences found in ethnographic essays and media critiques, and summarize research that takes up the intersectional approach in studying media experiences of Black audiences. Throughout the chapter, I will refer to "screen culture," first because most of her work focuses on film and television, and second because we experience so much media through screens—whether on cell phones, in theaters, or computers. The second part of the chapter will wrestle with hooks' contention that both dominant and black-oriented media often imagine and market products to a limited and stereotyped audience. Here, I mine her interviews with filmmakers and her film criticism to excavate a crucial argument that illuminates the important roles media critics can play for audiences and producers. Critics can educate audiences by helping them to see in new ways, preparing them for texts that challenge dominant representations. Media critics can also contribute to re-imagining existing audiences so that they are recognizable to producers as ready for different media texts. hooks' intervention adds to other scholars' discussions of how audiences are treated as commodities, even as their "active" characteristics are acknowledged—and exploited—by commercial media.

The third part of the chapter turns to hooks' contention that media representations are integral to individual and community recovery and solidarity. Her discussions of media depictions of poverty and black youth will be a focus here, along with her autoethnographic remembrances about the important aesthetic experiences of her childhood in the segregated south. The final part of the chapter reflects on the opening quotation, in concert with some criticism of hooks that she is imposing her standards on other people's choices and renders judgment on audiences without sufficient evidence of effects. I grant that, in some of her essays, hooks paints with broad strokes the impact of dominant images and narratives, describing youth or whites as under the influence in a manner consistent with "hypodermic needle"-type diagnoses. However, I will suggest that some of these passages are meant to provoke discussion and introspection rather than to condemn any particular group to zombie-like complacency. Additionally, I will argue that even though some of her descriptions are heavy-handed, they do resonate with some research in priming, framing, and implicit attitudes (IAT) that suggest the majority of the population are, at the very least, unconsciously affected by racial and sexual stereotypes. Thus, her provocations regarding what we consume in media and how it impacts our perceptions of each other provide opportunities to reflect, as well as to reinforce the connection between the personal and the political so integral to her vision of cultural and social transformation.

Audience Reception and Intersections

bell hooks' approach to audiences and communication resonates with the eth-nographically influenced audience studies that emerged in the 1980s and 1990s. Her investment in applying intersectional analysis to explorations of how people cull meaning from texts has inspired and augmented research that broke new ground in Communication Studies. hooks recognizes that people interact with media on multiple levels and in different contexts; they bring an array of life experiences, political attitudes, and expectations to encounters with media. She is most concerned with how people negotiate media texts that reinforce dominator culture; hooks wants to know how, when, and if audience members resist the oppressive messages about themselves and their fellow citizens that often dominate mainstream media. Specifically, she considers how, when, and whether media provide transformative moments for individuals and communities, moments when, to borrow from James Baldwin, we feel our dungeon shake and glimpse a different facet of freedom, agency, and self-hood that counters status quo hierarchies. She is suspicious of studies that try to separate the political aspects of media consumption from the pleasurable ones. Having herself experienced sublime, eye-opening moments with texts that changed her thinking, hooks challenges us to ask if our popular culture provides everyone with opportunities to re-imagine our existence.

Ien Ang is one of the most eloquent chroniclers of the reception studies turn in critical media studies. She describes how scholars in the mid-1980s were inspired by feminist, anti-racist, and neo-Marxist responses to empirical studies of audiences that positioned them as passive.[2] Many scholars turned to Stuart Hall's "Encoding/Decoding" framework to develop other models of audiences as participants in media culture. Audiences create and negotiate interpretive strategies as they encounter media, sometimes resisting preferred meanings, sometimes incorporating dominant ideologies into their lives with some twist. For Ang and others, the goal of audience studies is not to valorize any and all evidence of audience activity—contrasted with the passive audience depicted in past studies. Rather, one important goal is to explore

> how people live within an increasingly media-saturated culture, in which they have to be active (as choosers and readers, pleasure seekers and interpreters) in order to produce any meaning at all out of the overdose of images thrown before us.[3]

hooks' work is part of this paradigm shift, exploring how, in particular, Black audiences navigate the new array of "multicultural" images that have accumulated since the civil rights movement. Arguing that experiences of oppression and resis-

---

2. Ang, *Living Room Wars*.
3. Ang, *Living Room Wars*, 13.

tance shaped people's media consumption and interpretive practices, she examines the personal and political implications of media spectatorship, and the limits of "positive" imagery in a still-oppressive society. From the rubrics of black feminist thought, hooks' writings imply that studying audiences is only meaningful when such studies help us see how everyday habits of cultural consumption inflect and are inflected by politics. She posits that media consumption can also be seen as a moment of encounter with Others we may never, or rarely, approach off screen. Starting from the experiences of people whose images were rarely available and often distorted, being a spectator is far from apolitical. For hooks, centering the experiences of Black female audiences—grounded in a context of understanding, and expecting, racism, sexism, and hostility—means the moment of consumption isn't all about pleasure or control: it's about confrontation as well.

Confronting Oppression on Screen: Theorizing Black Audiences and Resistance

In her autoethnographic essays, interviews with friends and family, and descriptions of interactions with colleagues and students, hooks outlines how theorizing about media can flourish within homeplaces, schools, and other venues. Across multiple spaces, people share their outrage, relief, disbelief, and dismay about the quality and impact of images and narratives in wide circulation. What seems central to her contention is that black people (and in her examples, women in particular) had so little access to unambiguously *pleasurable* or empowering screen interpretations of blackness in dominant media outlets. To preserve their sense of dignity and positive self-esteem, resistant viewing was a necessary development for self-empowerment. This is not to say that all Black people developed this skill, or that Black people are born with the skill; rather, this indicates that the political and cultural conditions of the Jim Crow era made it more likely that Black people would develop a resistant standpoint on television and film as part and parcel of developing oppositional consciousness. There were few media "seductions" that did not require them to swallow a vicious stereotype.

hooks notes that the first generation of black moviegoers quickly realized that engaging in the "fun" of cinema meant entering a world of images generated by white supremacist logic. Thus, going to the movies—unless one was fortunate to live in an urban area where the films of Oscar Micheaux or the Johnson Brothers might be at a black-only theater—meant "to engage [cinema's] negation of black representation."[4] This necessitated a different kind of spectatorship than that engendered in white middle class audiences, who found themselves represented in an array of spectacles and situations. Oppositional spectatorship, critical reading, and questioning of the images, hooks suggests, was a necessary means of self-preservation for many black audience members. Interrogating rather than accepting

---

4. hooks, *Reel to Real*, 255.

the images of black inferiority was a part of anti-racist struggle on intimate and public grounds. Indeed, Anna Everett's comprehensive history of black film critics demonstrates how black opposition to racism in cinema emerged concurrently with the new medium.[5] In newspaper columns and magazine reviews, these early writers countered the racist fantasies on the silver screen and advocated for black independent filmmaking to foster better representations of black life.

Beyond professional criticism, hooks discusses the implicit and explicit training she and others received as they encountered screen culture and were encouraged to see links between the real world and the images conveyed on television and in movie theaters. At a time when looking at a white person "the wrong way" could lead to a lynching, watching white people on television was yet another place to learn about looking at them, and a place to be critical in a safe(r) space than the street. hooks argues it "was one way to develop critical spectatorship. . .you learned to look at white people by staring at them on the screen. Black looks, as they were constituted in movements for racial uplift, were interrogating gazes."[6] In *Yearning*, she recalls "vivid memories of watching the *Ed Sullivan Show* on Sunday nights, of seeing on that show the great Louis Armstrong. Daddy, who was usually silent, would talk about the music, the way Armstrong was being treated, and the political implications of his appearance."[7]

Here, spectatorship isn't passive, but agentic, providing a space within dominant culture where Black people could question the actions and motives of whites and re-vision whiteness not as all-powerful and controlling. Looking at Armstrong interacting in the scripted environment of network TV, she and her father engaged in a discussion about the parameters of his appearance, encouraging her to look beyond the surface of the shiny images and excavate the underlying power relations and constraints shaping the great jazz artist's performance in a white-dominated forum. She quotes Stuart Hall, who saw critical spectatorship as a means to reconceptualize white dominance as an "extrinsic force, whose influence can be thrown off like the serpent sheds its skin."[8] This redefinition allows for further interrogation of racial hierarchy—white dominance is not "natural" and unchangeable—and means to learn "to look [at media] a certain way in order to resist" dominator culture.[9] Being a spectator—learning to look—in this framework isn't limited to voyeuristic pleasures or fantasy of being like or with the characters on screen. Paraphrasing Manthia Diawara, hooks suggests that resistant viewers may feel a kind of power and experience subjectivity when they experi-

5. Everett, *Returning the Gaze*.
6. hooks, *Reel to Real*, 255–56.
7. hooks, *Yearning*, 3.
8. Stuart Hall quoted in hooks, *Reel to Real*, 255.
9. hooks, *Reel to Real*, 255.

ence moments of "rupture" as they resist identifying completely with the perspective of a film's dominant discourse.[10]

hooks contrasts the experience-based theorizing and resistance of Black female audiences with prominent feminist film theories of spectatorship. In particular, she discusses how Laura Mulvey's generative theory of the patriarchal cinematic gaze and female spectatorship overlooked the complications race and class bring to women's experiences with film. Mulvey posited that cinematic pleasures are experienced in two basic ways: pleasure from looking at others (voyeurism) and pleasure via identification with a "'mirrored' Other" in order to understand one's own identity.[11] She then argued that women's pleasures were displaced by the "split between active/male and passive/female" characterizations on screen, thereby allowing women to identify with passive characterizations of the female self, always the object of a male gaze rather than the subject. hooks remarks that Black female filmgoers didn't necessarily identify with either the passive/female or active/male sides of this binary, because both were almost always white and "such identification was disenabling."[12] Indeed, when looking at whites on screen, most Black women were aware not only of the stars, but also of the "supporting" figures of Black servants, mammies, and so forth who were in the film to "enhance and maintain white womanhood as object of the phallocentric gaze."[13] Thus, hooks concludes, Black women were more likely to view films "with an awareness of the way in which race and racism determined the visual construction of gender [and]. . . assumed white women knew it too."[14] With no "natural" or affirming point of identification on screen, Black women created spaces to deconstruct the power dynamics of white patriarchal gazes. Mainstream feminist film critics, hooks argues, didn't take into account that female spectators could use race, not just gender, as a starting point from which to criticize patriarchal dominance of film, or that women of color might experience pleasure of a different sort via disrupting dominant narratives through the intersection of race/gender.

But these screen encounters could also be painful, even if empowering in terms of fostering critical habits of mind. Knowing that gazes aren't passive, but are instead active, powerful spaces does not protect one from being "captured" by another's gaze or having yours misinterpreted. Emmett Till was killed for looking at a white woman by white men who used his look as an excuse to reassert their power. hooks and her sisters were cautioned to avoid looking directly at white men who drove past them for fear the men might take their gaze as an invitation to sexual assault.[15] And even with a nascent critical consciousness, watching por-

10. Ibid., 256.
11. Mulvey, "Visual Pleasure and Narrative Cinema."
12. hooks, *Reel to Real*, 263.
13. Ibid., 258.
14. Ibid., 263.
15. hooks, *Yearning*, 4.

trayals of black women in the 1950s and 1960s was often frustrating and sorrow-ful. For example, hooks recounts how she and her sisters cried, anguished at the fate of the young mulatta character, Peola, in *Imitation of Life*. Later, in an essay, she articulated what she and her sisters felt then as frustration through the lens of race/gender analysis: "[Peola] was tragic because there was no place in the cinema for her, no loving pictures. . . . We cried all night for you, for the cinema that had no place for you, we stopped thinking it would one day be different."[16] hooks chose, in revisiting this film and continuing to be a spectator, to interrogate the movies rather than "be hurt by the absence of black female presence."[17]

These experiences of rupture, confrontation, and critique can result in an ambivalent relationship to screen culture. For black women in particular, the consistent interruptions caused by "cinematic racism" often result in a rejection of cinema. Instead of subjecting oneself over and over again to racist and sex-ist visions of oneself and/or one's community, many black women give up on cinema as a space of pleasure. Remaining a movie fan is a complex decision for a Black to make when the majority of movies still ignore, degrade, or belittle their identity groups. "Every Black woman I spoke with who was/is an ardent movie goer. . .testified that to experience fully the pleasure of that cinema she had to close down critique, analysis; she had to forget racism."[18] That is, to be "seduced" by the dominant images offered in Hollywood films or mainstream television, black women and men often have to accept the rules of racial domination and "forget" how to be critical, at least for the duration of the show.

hooks is concerned about this willingness to subjugate oneself to racism and sexism, even temporarily, to receive the pleasures of a film scripted within domi-nant norms. She is especially concerned that now that the everyday and overt racial violence of the Jim Crow era has retreated, new generations of spectators are not being encouraged to be vigilant when looking at the screen. Too often, she argues, the frustration over not being able to control Black images leaves people "feeling weary, dispirited, and sometimes just plain old brokenhearted."[19] And these feelings of despair may lead to gaps of "mindless complicity" with the im-ages that continue to "mock and ridicule blackness."[20] How, then, in an era of multicultural or "post-racial" media production and consumption, do scholars and activists convey the continuing need for critical media literacy? This is an especially urgent question at a time when audience "activity" is celebrated and the Internet is offered as a solution to all problems of speech and representation, let alone the fact that most people—Black or otherwise—"do not want to think

16. hooks, *Reel to Real*, 262.
17. Ibid.
18. Ibid., 260.
19. hooks, *Black Looks*, 4.
20. Ibid., 6.

critically about why they can sit in the darkness of theaters and find pleasure in images" that dehumanize blackness.[21]

One key lesson hooks wants to teach is that the homegrown media criticism she and others learned was not a "natural" response to racism on screen. Rather, parents and elders chose to enter into conversations about the screen. Fostering critical spectatorship is a choice people make in spaces constructed as places for resistance and recovery. Seeing the development of critical spectatorship as a "natural" outgrowth of oppression or parental nurturance fails to recognize "the realm of choice, and the remarkable re-visioning of. . .the idea of 'home' that black women consciously exercised in practice."[22] The contributions of everyday resistance to political projects should not be dismissed because it devalues the active role of parents—mostly women—who teach "critical consciousness in domestic space."[23] Recovering these modes of resistance that occur outside of the public eye is important, because it reminds us to revisit spectatorship across a range of contexts in order to better understand when and where critical viewers are being encouraged—or discouraged—to see below the surface. We can't assume that racial identity or gender or class will magically bestow critical faculties; rather, in communities that make resistance a priority, habits of mind and critical practices are woven into everyday life such that individuals can find and sustain oppositional thought.

Active Black Audiences and Intersectional Analysis in Communication Studies

The black feminist approaches that hooks and others have outlined have influenced many media researchers. A growing number of studies have leveraged the intersectional, grounded theories of identity to pose questions about audience experiences and political realities. Ethnographic, qualitative approaches have produced nuanced, complex portraits that support many of hooks' conjectures about critical spectatorship and resistance.

One Black audience practice that researchers have illustrated is the tendency to draw upon cultural heritage, experience, and oppositional thought to "fill in the blanks" of texts that obscure or ignore a variety of Black experiences. For example, Jacqueline Bobo's study of Black women viewers of *The Color Purple* illuminated how women who had read the original Alice Walker text interwove their knowledge of the deeper depictions in the book into their movie experience. Despite the fact that many reviewers found the movie's rendering of black women and men disappointing, these women leveraged their relationship to the book to

21. Ibid., 5–6.
22. hooks, *Yearning,* 45.
23. Ibid., 47.

create a pleasurable, empowering narrative experience.[24] Likewise, participants responding to mainstream news coverage of the Million Man March applied their understanding of race relations, history, and culture to leaven the anemic and simplistic renderings of black public opinion in news magazines.[25]

The ambivalent relationship hooks describes between Black women and media is borne out in other audience studies. Robin Means Coleman's interviews with Black female and male viewers of 1980s and 1990s Black sitcoms revealed the mixed feelings African Americans have about the expanding set of shows and characters that have emerged since the popularity of *The Cosby Show*.[26] Jhally and Lewis' focus group study of *Cosby Show* viewers found Black participants wary of the ways in which people spoke about the Huxtable/Cosby family's success and its meaning for questions of racial equality.[27] Other scholars have found a range of skeptical reactions to contemporary Black-oriented media. Black interviewees expressed concerns about whether sitcoms update and re-circulate harmful stereotypes, and felt that independent Black media are necessary to counter racism in mainstream media.[28]

The ability to find and choose alternatives continues to be a key element of many black spectators' habits. Gwendolyn Osbourne's study of Black women romance readers found joyous responses to the emergence of Black-oriented romance novels. Women expressed relief to finally read love stories that didn't always center on white characters and communities. One reader (who is also a romance author) said, "I was in heaven when the black romances came out. You no longer had to pretend that you were the character with long, flowing blonde tresses."[29] Other scholars show how Black spectators use Black-oriented media to critique racism, to reinforce a sense of racial identity or pride, and to gain knowledge from positive Black role models.[30] Similarly, a handful of ethnographic studies of Black youth and hip hop find that the genre provides a source of cultural pride and cultural capital,[31] but that youth are also critical of misogynistic strains within the genre.[32]

Another recurrent finding about black audiences' activity is that most African American media consumers continue to be concerned about third-person effects—that is, they fear that white (or Asian or Latina/o) viewers will believe that

24. Bobo, *Black Women as Cultural Readers*.
25. Owens, "Media Messages, Self-Identity and Race Relations."
26. Means Coleman, *African American Viewers and the Black Situation Comedy*.
27. Jhally and Lewis, *Enlightened Racism*.
28. See these essays in *Say It Loud!* for examples: Inniss and Feagin, "The Cosby Show: The View From the Black Middle Class," Cornwell and Orbe, "Keepin' it Real" and/or "Sellin' Out to the Man"; Squires, "Black Audiences, Past and Present."
29. Osbourne, "Women Who Look Like Me," 65.
30. Fisherkeller, "It's Just Like Teaching People."
31. Berry and Manning-Miller, eds. *Mediated Messages and African-American Culture*; Carter. *Keepin' It Real*.
32. Mahiri and Conner, "Black Youth Violence Has a Bad Rap."

stereotypical media portrayals of Blacks are accurate and that this will affect how they treat Black people in the real world.[33] Their fears are warranted. Studies of local news, music videos, and even video games suggest that white viewers who consume dominant media: are likely to judge Black women more unfavorably than white women; tend to over-identify African American men as threatening or criminal; and reiterate stereotypes that Black people are less intelligent, more lazy or prone to welfare dependence than whites.[34] Indeed, experimental research results find many audience members will "remember" a suspect as Black even when news stories don't supply racial identifiers in crime news.[35]

It is not only qualitative studies that produce similar results to hooks' writings. Experimental and survey work that attend to intersections of race, class, gender, and age also resonate with her depictions of how group identities shape spectator experiences. In some of these quantitative studies, researchers have explored whether or not a stronger sense of black identity has an effect on one's perceptions or endorsement of media messages and/or outlets. Work that examines the impact of the intersections of gender and race suggests that Black women who have a more positive sense of racial identity are less likely to be negatively affected by thin-ideal media messages. On the other hand, a study of Black teenagers suggests that strong identification with Black characters on TV leads to stronger self-esteem, but heavy viewing of sports lowers self-esteem, as does identification with white lead characters.[36]

The idea that consuming black-oriented media "protects" black viewers from some kinds of racial harm is also supported by survey work by Richard Allen. Allen's study of 551 African Americans in the Detroit area found that greater consumption of Black print media led to increases in respondents' sense of Black autonomy, feelings of closeness to other Blacks, and African self-consciousness.[37] However, exposure to Black television and films led to a decrease in Black autonomy and African consciousness. Allen also noted that younger respondents tended to watch more Black media than older participants and felt closer to both the Black masses and elites, while older participants consumed more print media and felt a greater sense of ethnic identity, African self-consciousness, and Black autonomy. These results suggest that there are complex relationships between Black identity, gender, Black media consumption, and age, lending additional credence to hooks' emphasis on always considering the intersections of identities when we do research or think about applied interventions.

---

33. Means Coleman, *African American Viewers and the Black Situation Comedy*; Means Coleman, ed. *Say It Loud!*; Squires, *African Americans and the Media*; Berry and Miller, *Mediated Messages*.
34. E.g., Busselle and Crandall, "Television Viewing and Perceptions About Race Differences"; Gan, Zillmann, and Mitrook, "Stereotyping Effect of Black Women's Sexual Rap"; Entman and Rojecki, *The Black Image in the White Mind*.
35. Dixon and Azocar, "Priming Crime and Activating Blackness; Oliver and Fonash, "Race and Crime in the News."
36. Ward, "'Wading Through the Stereotypes.'"
37. Allen, *The Concept of Self: A Study of Black Identity*.

Activating Audiences in a Post-Civil-Rights World

Although she encourages readers to learn from and consider the tactics of the generations of resistant viewers she invokes, like Ang, hooks is suspicious of studies that suggest *any* type of active audience engagement will lead to progressive political outcomes or resistance. Particularly, hooks is concerned that Black people today are not gaining the same sort of critical viewing habits her community cultivated in the Jim Crow era. When a new generation is invited to participate in a "multicultural," post–civil–rights, post-feminist media environment, she asks: are resistant reading faculties now harder to cultivate? Since marketers are eager to target new "segments" previously shunned, people of color, LGBT, and other groups find themselves with a new array of choices. hooks worries that the seductions of equality through consumption and the "positive" portrayals of success via assimilation will not so readily generate the types of home-grown media criticism she learned as a child. She worries that some people, having experienced the newfound opportunities and luxuries afforded from assimilation/integration, may see ignoring racism or sexism as "the price of the ticket." Others subscribe to the notion that "race doesn't matter" anymore, "even as they labor to be as much like their white peers as possible" rather than embrace racial difference and cultural heritage as positive, generative elements of identity.[38] And, at a time when it's "hip" to "play" with stereotypes in humor, drama, and art, some people argue that "we're all racist"; thus, no one can claim any high ground to criticize racial representations that denigrate other groups. This type of argument ignores the fact that even if *all* people have internalized racism or hold racist beliefs about other groups, only a choice few groups—whites, for instance—have access to disproportionate power and privilege to curtail other people's life chances via racial reasoning. The idea that we're all affected by racism (or sexism, or homophobia) can "deflect attention away from or even excuse the oppressive, dehumanizing impact of white supremacy," and displaces questions of accountability, responsibility, and empowering oneself to make change.[39]

As in her discussions of the limits of characterizing media representations as "positive" or "negative," hooks asks us to rethink how even pleasurable images that convey higher status to some members of marginalized groups can serve to divert our attention from the continued issues of inequality and domination that adversely affect most members of those same groups. Whether audiences "participate" more with a wider range of choices is not the key issue for hooks. As Black

---

38. hooks, *Black Looks*, 17.

39. Ibid. 14–15. hooks is clear, as is her colleague Cornel West, to distinguish between people who take on the role and habits of victimhood and those who are victimized. hooks is not one to deny that people are victimized by racist, sexist, and homophobic acts, policies, stereotyping, etc., and that those acts and processes have material results—sometimes deadly results. However, she and West try to articulate how people have, can, and should adopt resistant frameworks for understanding and struggling with the context of domination. See their dialogues in *Breaking Bread* for many examples of the distinctions they make between internalizing a victim identity and acknowledging and resisting victimization.

pop culture and black audiences are commodified, how do these new relations of media production, consumption, and circulation shape how black people look at media? There are more choices, but as Ang writes, "'choices' is by definition an open-ended, procedural mechanism—it can be manipulated but not imposed— [and] there can be no guarantee people will" resist or reinforce status quo relations of power or discourses as they "make space" to interpret (and increasingly create) media.[40] If hooks is correct in figuring critical spectatorship as an engine of self-determination and self-preservation for marginalized people, then we may well be worried about the seductiveness of commercial media's framework for choice making, which can obfuscate how racism and sexism operate. Here is where media critics can play a role, being bold in their writing and speaking to the political implications of images, as well as the potential benefits of alternative, radical texts that reimagine and challenge ideas of race, sex, and class.

Learning to See: Critics, Audiences, Media Literacy, and Imagination

One can learn things without knowing it and without knowing what one has learned.[41]
—*Ramsey Eric Ramsey*

We learn how to "read" the interplay between image and sound on screen much as we learn how to read words imprinted on paper. Spectatorship, however, is not taught in school or in the loving increments of trial and error efforts children exert under adult tutelage. Growing up in Western screen culture, we learn to distinguish the laugh track from the laughter of actors. We understand that the hapless teen couples don't hear the ominous music welling in the background foreshadowing their doom in horror movies, and that the black guy usually gets killed first. We have also learned what types of people usually fill various roles: we recognize the kinds of people who are "leading men," heroes and heroines, villains and sidekicks, desired or mocked. Not until these dominant aesthetic and narrative conventions are poorly executed, spoofed, or directly questioned do we realize how much we have learned to understand, interpret, and expect particular configurations of sound and image. Until the normative flow is interrupted, we forget how fluent we've become in the language of wide-angle shots, close-ups, and other techniques of framing dramatic and comedic action on screen.

When we hear that a movie has cast its lead actors "against type"—the ways that race, gender, and nationality frame producer and audience expectations become obvious—what we have "learned" to expect, to make sense in terms of populating the screen, is articulated in explicit terms. When Asian American actors hear from casting agents that directors don't "see them as leading man material"

---

40. Ang, *Living Room Wars*, 12.
41. Ramsey, "Somehow, Learning to Live: On Being Critical," 90.

or "romantic lead" material, we can see that many people have been conditioned to expect members of the dominant racial groups to continue leading and being the focus of narratives of desire and triumph.[42] We understand that casting agents and media producers using their own expectations and assumptions about what the audience will find "authentic" or "realistic" can easily reinforce already-existing stereotypes and continue unequal relations and opportunities in screen culture. When public discussions of the success or failure of "casting against type" occur, we can more easily see other options as well as the assumptions that have kept types so racially segregated for so long. However, the conventions of realism used in most mainstream media work against highlighting the conventions of production, or how we represent "real world" situations. Not all media texts announce their intentions, so we may need prompting to reconsider why and what we have seen.

For hooks, then, critics serve

> to illuminate something that is already there. For example, the contemporary movie *Crash*, I thought was a very weak statement about race and class. That was already in the film. What I did in having a conversation about it was illuminate why it was a weak analysis.[43]

Critics of screen culture can leaven our education as spectators. They can influence how we imagine the range of films, television shows, or video games we might sample or avoid. While criticism is not the sole determinant of what audiences consume, critics are part of the process of audience identification and audience building. From advance film screenings held for critics to spark conversations in other media to the ubiquitous blurbs plastered on ads for new shows, to websites such as Rottentomatoes.com, critics send signals to audiences about what types of aesthetic experiences they will have, what to expect, and what fits their tastes. Media producers rely upon a mix of professional and lay critics (the latter of which multiply by the minute online) to get the right kind of "buzz" going about their work, especially if the producer does not have unlimited advertising budgets or staff to make and circulate publicity. Critics do some of the work of preparing audiences for what they will see, and bell hooks argues that more critical cultural writers should engage in preparing audiences to see in new ways. When hooks speaks of film criticism, though, she is not only talking about the work done by the folks who assign stars or give a thumbs up in a Sunday column; she is also referring to the criticism done in academia. She is troubled by the fact that many media arts programs do not require or teach films outside of European and white American traditions, and that in the journals and specialty publications

---

42. Ono and Pham, *Asian Americans and Media*; Adachie, Director, *The Slanted Screen*.
43. Lowens, "How Do You Practice Intersectionality?"

for academics and filmmakers, too few works by people of color and women are even discussed.[44]

As discussed in Chapter Three, dominant screen culture has tutored audiences in specific ways of seeing people of color and women. hooks notes how even those viewers who yearn for images that break stereotypes and move to new ground can have a hard time finding and/or getting acquainted with alternative and independent media. Even when people actively resist conventional screen representations and empower themselves with critical viewing habits, more may be required to appreciate films or videos that re-imagined female, LGBT, or black heterosexual lives. She recounts how her sisters initially reacted to their forays into foreign films: they hated them. They were incensed, initially, that they had to do more work to negotiate subtitles and not just be entertained, "a violation of Hollywood notions of spectatorship."[45] Later, hooks interviewed her sisters after they had become appreciative of foreign films. One told her that she had come to enjoy and seek out foreign films more because she had "learned that there was more to looking than I had been exposed to in ordinary [Hollywood] movies." She agreed with hooks that the alternative films they saw—even those focused on white people—were different because they demystified whiteness rather than re-normalizing or glamorizing whiteness.[46]

hooks insists that critics can and should play a larger role in preparing people for different screen experiences and encouraging them to try out novel cinematic texts. This is necessary to give a fighting chance to screen texts created explicitly to challenge or undermine the status quo renderings of marginalized groups. For these films to "make magic"—pulling the viewer into an intimate, wondrous suspension of disbelief—they require a different alchemy that the dominant Hollywood model provides. hooks discussed the need to prepare audiences with filmmaker Charles Burnett, referring to the importance of carefully written advance publicity and preparation that helped bring audiences to Julie Dash's breakthrough *Daughters of the Dust*.

> bell hooks: In the future, critics and black filmmakers need to be engaged more with each other. . . . There have got to be more spaces where an audience can creatively approach the work. Public response to *Daughters of the Dust* showed us that you can create an audience, you can prepare an audience that has been addicted to seeing movies in certain ways.[47]

This reflection on the role of the critic is an important intervention into the chicken-and-egg logic of commercial media: newcomers and activists are often

44. See, for example, her comments about most film students' lack of knowledge of key African American filmmakers such as Charles Burnett and Haile Gerima, in her interview with Burnett in *Reel to Real*, 194–214.
45. hooks, *Reel to Real*, 269.
46. Ibid.
47. Ibid., 210–11.

told there is no audience for the kinds of media they want to produce, thus it isn't worth the risk to invest. hooks acknowledges their profit concerns, but returns to the notion that "audiences are made" not born.[48] It is not fair or logical, for instance, to expect filmmakers who break with the 100-year-old conventions of Hollywood aesthetics to have evidence of a paying audience. Thus, Dash's team created packets of historical information, talked with critics, and gave them tools with which they could approach this material about black women in the South that broke with so many conventions of how to depict Black women in the nineteenth century.[49] Dash helped prepare mainstream critics and others to teach audiences how to see the film through different expectations, different historical lenses on Black American culture. For hooks, this kind of effort not only helps build audiences, but also widens the circle of people who support the premise that it is necessary to diversify screen culture in order to "decolonize our minds" from race and gender oppression. Fostering discussion of how progressive films work, and how they may help us see the variety within (as well as between) identity groups, is one way cultural critics can impact audiences, hopefully enhancing their media literacy skills and ability to advocate for alternative media.

Media Literacy: Marketable "Skills" and Meaningful Criticism

To hooks, coming to consciousness is, in part, coming to see oneself as empowered to struggle, even if one is not optimistic regarding the likely outcomes of any given moment of resistance to make immediate change to socioeconomic inequalities. Being critical of media is one type of everyday practice that can help sustain oppositional consciousness and foster solidarity. Thus, being "media literate" is not just about having the skills to navigate the multiplying pathways of media culture, but also about having the skills to leverage one's literacy in the service of communal struggles against domination. hooks' insistence on applying critical media literacy in the political realm dovetails with a recent essay by Sonia Livingstone about the varying uses and definitions of the term "media literacy." Arguably, in her work as a film critic and as a teacher, hooks has fostered media literacy to help people deconstruct dominant media discourses. However, her linkage between literacy and oppositional consciousness implies what types of media literacy efforts she would suggest and those she would find suspicious. The question becomes: media literacy in the service of whose goals?

Livingstone argues that media literacy may be a more fertile framework for thinking through the implications of new media technologies and consumption/ production than audience studies. Literacy as a term invokes both reading and writing (consumption and production); it suggests active engagement and skills

---

48. Ibid., 209.
49. Dash, *Daughters of the Dust*; hooks, *Reel to Real*, 214.

that are learned and refined.[50] However, within the framework of public education and government regulation of media industries, media literacy is often invoked as a means of protecting or improving a vulnerable sector of the audience/public. These invocations also have classist overtones that suggest the media "illiterate" are part of a problematic, lower class that will require intensive tutoring to become literate enough to manage modern life, further stigmatizing those who lack the cultural capital of already literate groups.[51] Importantly, discussions of programs to create media literacy amongst youth or other "vulnerable" populations (ostensibly victims in waiting) often intersect with plans to deregulate media industries. Here, "media literacy" becomes a neoliberal-friendly way of saying, as long as "active" audiences educate themselves, no regulation is needed because they will make "the right choices" as empowered individuals.[52]

Commercial media outlets try to stay a step ahead of the active audience by anticipating and shaping desires. When audiences seek "the right choices," they are confronted with an array of media that have been concocted by marketing plans, tested with focus groups and other pre-determined mechanisms to identify a target group. Oftentimes, racial and gender identities are used as part of the profiling. Oscar Gandy's recent work on audience segmentation via "profiles" that include race/ethnicity resonates with hooks' concern that in the new media environment, neither multicultural-esque visions of new market shares nor finer delineations of tastes and desires by newfangled surveillance tools are bound to "tailor" content to Black or other audiences of color that breaks with the status quo.[53] Gandy notes that segmentation of audiences isn't inherently bad—folks self-identify and gather around group identities all the time to take in a play or support a new film, etc., based on a sense of shared affinities, political interests, and "linked fate." When, for example, someone such as hooks, or a director such as Spike Lee, urges black audiences to support new black filmmakers, it is from this sense of linked fate, of accountability, and desires to see more diversity in film. But segmentation also happens in ways inconsistent with the political and cultural aspects of group identification.

Gandy draws from C. Edwin Baker's notion of "corrupted diversity." Diversity is "corrupted" when distinctions that are drawn between groups aren't generated by the groups themselves or don't refer to their shared interests but rather are generated by the goals of external constituencies—marketers, political actors, and more. When outsiders "classify" race/ethnic groups without attention to those shared needs, linked fate, etc., the resultant media products are usually incongru-

---

50. Livingstone, "Engaging with Media—A Matter of Literacy?"
51. Ibid., 7–8.
52. Ibid., 9.
53. Gandy, "Matrix Multiplication and the Digital Divide."

ent with the political interests of the groups.[54] Moreover, the distinctions drawn through ever-increasingly sophisticated and intrusive marketing tools are done in order to differentiate between audience "profiles" that will generate the most profit. As Gandy writes, these distinctions "are used for one fundamental purpose—the enhancement of discriminatory choices regarding whose interests are to be met and whose needs are to be set aside. . .to identify targets for predation, or the marketing of harmful products."[55] Those whose needs are set aside are more likely to be lower income people of color, underscoring the problem that class and racial "disadvantage cumulates over time and space."[56]

Livingstone's cautions on the limits of literacy and Ang's observations about the vagaries of choice, joined together with Gandy's and hooks' concerns that the marketplace is still saturated with dominant racial imagery/discourses and low-quality information, recommend that folks get media literate in a specific way. That is, understanding "the importance of not reducing reception to an individualized, essentially psychological process, but to conceptualize it as a deeply politicized, cultural one."[57] Getting there requires educational resources, community support, small group discussions, and reflective thinking. And, for hooks, becoming critical is a vehicle to healing, to finding one's place in the world as an empowered being.

Reception and Self-Recovery

When bell hooks writes about self-esteem, mental health, and recovery, she is not trying to promote "magical thinking"—that just by changing our minds we will change everything.[58] Having suffered racism and sexism herself, she believes that each of us may require some individual healing as we confront and explore how dominator culture may have shaped our habits of mind and everyday practices. But hooks makes it clear that her interest in self-recovery is not in sync with that promoted in most best-selling self-help books and videos. She finds their approach too removed from socio-political contexts. As with her work on education, the writings of Buddhist teachers and critical scholars led her to define self-recovery as an ongoing process by which one recovers from alienation in order to be whole. Moreover, self-recovery should lead to participation in struggles against injustice so that everyone can be whole.[59] hooks considers this kind of personal-level transformation—always situated in community and in service of community—an integral part of political resistance. Self-recovery goes beyond naming one's pain or personal harm done by dominator culture; self-recovery occurs in part through sophisticated awareness and understanding of how institutions and

---

54. Gandy, 132–34.
55. Ibid., 140.
56. Ibid.
57. Ang, *Living Room Wars*, 137.
58. See critiques of magical thinking in Gunn and Cloud, "Agentic Orientation."
59. hooks, *Talking Back*, 29–30.

social forces affect one's life (the sociological imagination). This level of awareness helps one to heal and to begin to undertake strategies of resistance.[60]

Healing the self, the psyche, from racism/sexism/classism is a necessary foundation for challenging "existing negative stereotypes and reclaim[ing] [our] right to self-definition."[61] Critical spectatorship, then, and teaching critical media literacy to people, are practices of recovery; a type of outreach to those struggling to make sense of their marginalization. Becoming a critical spectator and engaging with others in conversation about media effects is a way to transform habits of mind that internalize domination and reinforce the dehumanization found so often in media spectacles. Rejecting and deconstructing media narratives that continue to depict blackness as hateful or women as sex objects is a movement towards "self-love" and care that creates room for people to imagine different paths to a better future. hooks, for example, exhorts black heterosexual men to engage in self-recovery in part by engaging the radical media produced by Black gay men such as Essex Hemphill and Marlon Riggs. To unlearn dominant patriarchal masculine models fostered in mainstream media, men must re-imagine their upbringing, their boyhood, and think differently about how to raise their children. hooks asks men to "dare to dream about masculinity that humanizes. They must dare to embrace boyhood as a time of wonder, play, and self-invention"[62] rather than a time of "hardening" oneself into a man who can assert his will to dominate others who cross him. Hemphill, Riggs, and writers such as Kevin Powell provide men with models for rethinking masculinity that include insightful critiques of the ways mainstream media reinforce the idea that black men are only "real men" when they are violent, heterosexual, and emotionally distant.

Media contribute so much to our imaginary worlds, desires, self-esteem, education, and experiences of pleasure. Media can also challenge or sully one's sense of self or community, sensibilities nurtured in homeplaces but not necessarily matched in other public spaces. hooks demonstrates this dynamic by contrasting how she experienced being poor as a child and how mainstream media influence how most people think about poor Americans. Growing up, poverty "was no disgrace. . . . We were socialized early on, by grandparents and parents, to assume nobody's value could be measured by material standards."[63] When she attended Stanford and encountered people who articulated the belief that the poor were shiftless and lazy, she drew upon her lessons from home to deconstruct their attitudes. However, such attitudes are reinforced by contemporary popular culture that "rarely represents the poor in ways that display integrity and dignity."[64]

---

60. Ibid., 32.
61. hooks, *We Real Cool*, 142.
62. Ibid., 144.
63. hooks, *Outlaw Culture*, 167.
64. Ibid., 168.

Moreover, hooks worries that many people today—poor and rich—internalize the dominant message that one's worth is equal to one's financial wealth. She argues that changing the representations of the poor, and resisting current representations, will have to be part of changing attitudes and policy. She links the over-representation of "liberal individualism, the idea that you make it by the privatized hoarding of resources, not by sharing them," with the dehumanization of the poor and lack of empathy and sense of accountability in the public sphere.[65] Thus, she advocates that scholars and activists fight the "dehumanizing system of representation" of the poor, which, she argues, engenders in many "a deep-seated crippling lack of self esteem."[66] If we consider our media literacy a resource, then "progressive literacy programs. . .could use popular movies as a base to begin learning and discussion" about the ways in which the depictions of poverty haven't done justice to the poor. "To change the face of poverty so it becomes, once again, a site for the formation of values. . .as any other class positionality in this society, we would need to intervene in existing systems of representation."[67]

Beyond rigid, simplistic notions of role modeling, we know that media influence our range of sensibilities. Thus, hooks is particularly interested in changing the media and cultural landscapes offered to children. Her children's books—*Happy to Be Nappy, Be Boy Buzz, Grump Groan Growl*—can be viewed as outgrowths of her theories of self-recovery: children, especially children of color, are harmed when they are deprived of nurturing aesthetic experiences. Media watchdog groups such as Children Now continue to find harmful stereotypes and evidence of effects on how children see people of color and themselves. hooks' arguments about representation and self-esteem post that kids are harmed when socialized into a dominator culture that artificially restricts their sense of self, of possibilities, of love. Given media culture's dependence on commercialism and the intensity of marketing to children through every genre and channel, from cartoons, to sci-fi, to sports, fostering in children a sense of wonder and self-worth not associated with the acquisition of consumer goods can be a challenge for any caregiver. For hooks, working to make alternative aesthetic experiences readily available to children is part of the process of healing and preventing hurt caused by sexist, classist, and racist media messages. Part of the project of critical media literacy, then, is reviving community-centered thinking that includes children and young adults early on, so folks aren't so wounded in the first place. Thus, hooks' turn to children's literature as a way to reach broader audiences and provide alternatives for children and those who care for them.

In her introduction to *Salvation: Black People and Love*, hooks recounts asking African American children to talk about love. She was distressed to hear their

---

65. Ibid. 171.
66. Ibid.
67. Ibid.

reply: love doesn't exist in this world. She characterizes their dismissal of love as evidence of how black children are,

> disenfranchised, neglected, or rendered invisible in this society. . . . Standing before black children who tell me there is no love in clear, flat, dispassionate voices, I confront our collective failure as a nation, and as African Americans, to create a world where we can all know love.[68]

These children and their communities had few resources—material, spiritual, imaginative—to understand love as hooks does. And, the symbolic annihilation of Black youth in media does not reflect what Cornel West defines as a "love ethic. . .self-love and love for others. . .modes towards increasing self-valuation and encouraging political resistance in one's community."[69] As explained in the previous chapters, hooks views mass media as one source of spiritual malaise, where people's self-esteem is bombarded by messages that we're not rich enough, or beautiful enough, and so on. The mainstream media offer few places for black children to feel love, to experience identifications with interesting, empowering visions of possible futures. The aesthetic worlds they encounter in dominant media rarely afford them sensual experiences that support deep listening, reflection, joy.

In her memoir, *Bone Black*, hooks recounts multiple instances when literature, dreams, gardens, and other aesthetic, sensory experiences helped her recover from unjust punishments, sexist religious dogma, and racist abuse. As a child, these experiences fed her imagination, and were augmented by observations of elders who seemed to have a magical connection to the seasons, the earth, the spirit world. She recalls her grandmother, whom she called Saru, teaching her stories of their family's past, legends from Native American culture, and how to honor the earth. Assisting Saru with chores, she gathered fresh eggs from the hens: "I am excited by this knowledge of where eggs really come from, by the smells in the chicken coop, by the sounds."[70] After being framed as an outcast who was too smart to be attractive to any sane man, she took solace reading about headstrong characters such as Jo Marsh in *Little Women* and felt "a little less alone in the world."[71]

Active Then, but Not Now?
Reflecting on bell hooks' Indictment of Contemporary Spectators

Some of bell hooks' critics assert that she writes in a way which suggests that only she and a handful of Black leaders can think about the world in the correct way.[72]

68. hooks, *Salvation: Black People and Love*, xix.
69. Quoted in *Salvation*, 5.
70. hooks, *Bone Black: Memories of Girlhood*, 59.
71. Ibid., 77.
72. In a review of *Rock My Soul*, E. Francis White commented, "Using some idiosyncratic and highly selective examples, she argues that endemic low self-esteem is the most serious issue facing black people today. She makes this argument as if she were the first black intellectual to seriously focus on the topic. She ignores the legions of black intellectuals

And, if we compare her depiction of the post–civil rights generation to her complex account of civil–rights–era Black women spectators as resistant, and resilient, readers of mainstream media, then hooks' account of the media's contribution to a rampant critical and self-esteem deficit seems off-base. Passages such as this, from her 2003 book *Rock My Soul: Black People and Self Esteem*, don't seem to be of a piece with her earlier work in *Reel to Real*:

> Any African-American who watches television for more than a few hours a week is daily ingesting toxic representations and poisonous pedagogy. Yet the ingestion of constant propaganda that teaches black people self-hate has become so much the norm that it is rarely questioned.[73]

This harsh diagnosis of viewers reads as a direct contradiction of the empowered, home-grown criticism she and others speak of when describing critical, active audiences. This excerpt, as well as her discussions of the impact of liberal materialism cited above, prompts the question: Why does she think the current generation of African Americans is so ill-equipped to question and critique images on TV? More to the point: this comment suggests that hooks hasn't engaged with literature cited in this chapter that suggests at least some type of critical consciousness is alive and well amongst African American audience members. Perhaps she is broad and blunt in her estimation of critical faculties of contemporary audiences to provoke discussion; however, in light of her own work and that which she has inspired, the ways she depicts the problems of audiences today are problematic. Too often in her commentary on audience perceptions she seems to juxtapose the past and present abilities of audiences without providing as many rich examples and anecdotes about the latter in comparison to the former. And, given the burgeoning sites for audience discussion online, one would hope that hooks would see ample evidence of the sorts of critical media dissection she yearns for happening everywhere from YouTube to listservs to Twitter, as well as on the websites of progressive organizations such as ColorofChange.org and MediaMatters.org.

Arguably, dominant representations of race continue to shape our psyches. Priming research and Implicit Attitudes Test (IAT) studies strongly suggest that people of all colors, for example, revert to anti-black stereotypes and patriarchal ideologies under certain conditions. Our media culture trains us to "see" Black men as threatening, women as natural nurturers, and white men as intellectual superiors.[74] However, the extent of the damage and recovery prospects vary across groups and individuals. While IAT tests show that we snap to the stereotypical judgments, research also shows that exposure to counter-stereotypical portrayals

and artists who have worked to counter low self-esteem: from Ralph Ellison to Gwendolyn Brooks; from Nina Simone to John Coltrane. . . ." "The Price of Success," 17–18.

73. hooks, *Rock My Soul*, 221.

74. See the exhaustive review of IAT studies by Jerry Kang, "Trojan Horses of Race."

and discussions can change people's attitudes under certain conditions.[75] Perhaps the fruits of the counter-hegemonic audience reactions have not yet been reaped in terms of political action, but the current prospects for critical audience activity certainly do not appear to be as bleak as hooks' recent writings seem to suggest.

---

75. Schiappa, *Beyond Representational Correctness*. See also work by the Frameworks Institute on changing public conversations about topics such as gender equity through re-framing. Descriptions of this work and its limits are available to the public at http://frameworksinstitute.org/ecd.html.

∿ Six ∿

Education As a
Tool for Democracy

Multiculturalism compels educators to recognize the narrow boundaries that have shaped the way knowledge is shared in the classroom. It forces us to recognize our complicity in accepting and perpetrating biases of any kind.[1]

As in her writings on media, bell hooks draws upon her own experiences in the classroom—both as a student and as a professor—to explore the dynamics of teaching and learning. This grounded theory approach produces a critique aimed at re-thinking the modes and aims of education in a society that aspires to pluralism. Especially in the books *Teaching to Transgress* and *Teaching Community*, she outlines a theory of education as democratic liberatory practice. Knitting together autoethnography, educational psychology, black feminist theory, and liberation theologies born of progressive Black and Buddhist spiritual teachings, hooks' writings on education confront the operation of power and inequality in the classroom. She calls for transformational pedagogies that unify theory and practice. She states that "education as the practice of freedom is not just about liberatory knowledge, it's about liberatory practice in the classroom," practices that she understands to be crucial to reinvigorating our democracy.[2] To do so requires transformation of hegemonic modes of teaching and learning.

Hegemonic Habits: Rethinking the Classroom in Dominator Culture
Within dominator culture, teaching is often equated with "training" students who are passive vessels for the instructor's superior knowledge. Students are expected

---

1. hooks, *Teaching to Transgress*, 44
2. Ibid., 147.

to listen, to attend, to submit, and to prove their worth by following the commands of the professor. Students are expected to please their teachers and are not supposed to question their authority. Teachers then rank students in order of "ability" via grading and reward those students who do best with praise and high grades. In this system, hooks notes that many professors "think it normal to intimidate or shame students and create a competitive rather than collaborative atmosphere,"[3] which mirrors the dog-eat-dog competition of the marketplace. Students will often mimic their professors' habits, shaming their classmates and/ or viewing them as rivals for a professor's attention. This model positions professors as gatekeepers who evaluate the worth of students to share their knowledge; it is not assumed that teachers should aim to share knowledge with everyone. Thus, classroom is a competitive space where students compete and are divided into those who have the right stuff to excel, and those who are doomed to fall behind.

This competitive atmosphere and expectation of passivity from students is imbued with race, class, gender, and sexual politics. Until recently, people from particular raced, gendered, and classed groups have been excluded from historically white institutions of higher education. Moreover, cadres of scholars/professors theorized the inferiority and pathologies of these excluded people. Traditional research paradigms in the social sciences and humanities have objectified women, people of color, gays and lesbians. Thus, one task of liberatory multicultural education is to recognize and deconstruct the ways that students and professors of different racial, ethnic, or gender groups challenge the dominant paradigm. That is, once integration of educational institutions brings in formerly excluded and dehumanized students into the halls and classrooms, we need to ask: how will their presence—their differences—be understood and interact with the presuppositions of dominant models of education? For hooks, thinking about the actual embodiment—the bodies—of students and teachers in the academy is one necessary step in deconstructing the dominant paradigm.

Recognizing Our Material Selves in the Classroom

We have a lot of people who don't recognize that being a teacher is being with people.
—*Ron Scrapp*[4]

This epigraph encapsulates much of bell hooks' multifaceted critique of conventional academia and dominator culture. Dominant teaching norms draw from the same dualistic premises and power/knowledge matrices that hooks deconstructs in her work on racism and sexism. The mind/body dualism that is hegemonic in Western culture manifests in the classroom for teachers and learners. She notes

---

3. hooks, *Teaching Community*, 86.
4. hooks and Scrapp, "Building a Teaching Community," in *Teaching to Transgress*, 165.

that many people (and artifacts of popular culture) still cling to a "romantic notion of the professor [that] is so tied to a sense of the transitive mind, a mind that
is, in a sense, always at odds with the body."[5] White male professors—those
who have historically been privileged with access to intellectual personae that enable them to bifurcate body/mind—rarely have to worry that their bodies will be
objects of interest or conflict for students. Women and men of color, as well as
white women, on the other hand, are over-associated with the body in dominant
culture. Thus, when they enter the classroom, some may question their presence
or be likely to assess them based on appearance, whether they are students or
faculty. For example, students are more likely to comment on the appearance
or family status of female professors than male professors, and expect more caring behavior from white female teachers.[6] Black women are often perceived as
strong but domineering and loud, traits consistent with the Matriarch/Sapphire
stereotypes.[7]

The body/mind split plays out with respect to emotions as well: the "con-
trolled" body that does not display passion is considered more "objective" and "rational" than the bodies of teachers and learners who use more expressive gestures
or vocal tone, or who show their keen interest or investment in a topic. Part of a
liberatory pedagogy, then, comes from acknowledging the physicality and experiences of the people in the room, to recognize their wholeness as thinking, breath-
ing, feeling beings constituted in history and culture. This acknowledgment helps
to "disrupt the notion of the professor as omnipotent, all-knowing mind" and
paves the way for us to "deconstruct the way power has been traditionally orches-
trated in the classroom, denying subjectivity to some groups and according it to
others."[8] It can also make room for students to be more active in learning rather
than the conventional passivity. For example, when students and teachers connect
personal experiences to class topics, or engage in excited speech about theory, "our
collective passions come together, and there is often an emotional response. . . .
[But] the restrictive, repressive classroom ritual insists that emotional responses
have no place. . . the underlying assumption is you have to be cut off from your
emotions."[9] But it is often in that passionate, emotional moment that a student
or group of students finally "gets it"—finally makes historical facts or abstract
ideas matter and make sense in a profound way. Ignoring or suppressing emotion
can hamper learning, and can make for particularly bad pedagogical choices in
many fields, including Communication Studies. hooks' attention to the role of
emotions in the classroom is instructive for our field, given that the media are in

---

5. hooks, *Teaching to Transgress*, 137.
6. Ibid., 136–37. See also TuSmith and Reddy, eds. *Race in the College Classroom*; Stanley, "Coloring the Academic
Landscape."
7. Donovan, "Tough or Tender."
8. hooks, *Teaching to Transgress*, 139.
9. Ibid., 155.

the business of eliciting emotional reactions from the public: comedians want us to laugh; dramatists want us to cry; horror directors want us to fear the shadows on the wall; and politicians want us to feel patriotic. When we teach students to deconstruct these materials, we have to recognize that many of them will have emotional responses that will, quite possibly, affect how they engage with the process as well as the classroom atmosphere.

When I was a teaching assistant, one of the professors I worked for taught a unit on censorship. As part of the unit, he screened different sex scenes from Hollywood films—some humorous, some dramatic, and one depicting a violent rape—and then asked students to discuss whether proposed anti-pornography statutes would prohibit any of the movies from being released. I sat in the auditorium, shocked at the more graphic scenes, shown without discussion or warning. A few days later, a student disclosed to me that she was a survivor of sexual assault and did not want to return to class. Her experience of the material (and I expect the experiences of many of her classmates) was not one characterized by disembodied consideration of sex scenes and legal statutes; it was an experience of fear, anger, and exclusion. While neither hooks nor I would argue that professors should avoid showing provocative examples in class, it is possible and preferable to carefully plan how one will introduce such material, and to do so fully aware that the experiences of diverse students require us to think about the impact of the material when we use media in the classroom—texts created with the specific intent of arousing people's emotions. We must plan for and create space to allow students to process their emotional responses, to account for a variety of engagements with the material. This level of engagement, though, is rarely taught or explicitly discussed in conventional graduate programs that produce the bulk of the professoriate.

My example illustrates another point hooks makes in her discussions of pedagogy: sharing knowledge is an intimate experience that confounds the mind/body dualism of dominant culture. While each and every lesson plan won't contain such obvious instances of personal connection to materials, students put their trust in teachers every day. They open their minds, make themselves vulnerable to critique, and expose their weaknesses, as peers witness their struggles to understand and incorporate theory, facts, and figures. If we understand teaching and learning as intimate processes, then linking the personal and the intellectual is key to making learning *matter* to students. It also highlights how the relationship between teacher and students warrants careful development. For hooks, the classroom is a space where there are delicate balances to be struck between learners and instructors. There are emotions involved in learning: the joy of finally getting a theoretical concept; the shame in failing an exam; the anxiousness of the first day; nervousness when one dares to challenge the professor's interpretation. Thus, instructors need to carefully craft pedagogies to encourage community through mutual exchange and respect.

Mutuality and Respect in the Classroom

"In regards to pedagogical practices we must intervene to alter the existing peda-gogical structure and teach students *how to listen, how to hear one another.*"[10] This is a challenge, given how conventional educational practices overemphasize ca-reer- and future-oriented thinking, competition, and listening primarily to the in-structor as expert. To create an environment where students can engage in mutual exchange, we have to reconsider our habits of speaking, critiquing, grading, and lecturing. We can't just substitute in new "liberatory" or "multicultural" content and still deliver it in the same dominant ways. Students will not learn to question, or feel they're allowed to engage with the material or each other, unless we provide them with different avenues for dialogue and questioning. This might start with a basic reconsideration of the classroom's physical set up. hooks reminisces about the excitement she felt

> when I took my first class where the teacher wanted to change how we sat. . .to a circle where we could look at one another. That change forced us to recognize one another's presence. We couldn't sleepwalk our way to knowledge.[11]

In addition to reconfiguring the physical arrangements of a classroom, the value of mutuality elevates listening, reflection, and transformation. When students con-sider a controversial topic, traditional debate norms suggest taking up of distinct oppositional viewpoints in a contest to see who can make the best argument and defeat their opponent; conventional journalistic norms urge us to find "two sides to every story." These reinforce combative, dualistic approaches to thinking about issues, setting students up to see each other as enemies rather than as collaborators.

Beyond Two Sides: Practices for Facilitating Mutual Dialogue

Instructors should be creative, then, in finding ways to facilitate discussion, writ-ing assignments or classroom interactions that are not premised on dualism and competition. Offering ways for students to listen to each other, to contemplate multiple facets of an issue—not just the two most obvious "sides"—and to take time to reflect, are ways to practice habits of mind that are not grounded in domination of an Other. One example of this is the "think-pair-share" method of starting class discussion. Students first work alone, thinking about and jotting down their own ideas, opinions, and reasons for why they think a particular way about a concept or event. Then, in pairs, they share their ideas, taking turns listening to each other without counter-arguments or interruptions. Afterwards, the instructor can invite pairs to convey each other's ideas with the larger class,

---

10. Ibid., 150.
11. hooks, *Teaching to Transgress*, 146.

and begin a larger discussion, or continue the discussions within the dyads. Either way, the students have practiced different ways of relating to each other, to ideas, to discussion controversy. No one—including the instructor—is positioned as an expert or responsible for "winning" the argument, and no consensus is required to end the session.

Another way to challenge the dominant academic model is to change how students view personal experience as a means for approaching material in class. Many students become alienated from the books they read because they have to work so hard—often futilely—to make a clear connection between theory and everyday life, between the humanities' sometimes esoteric concerns with art or philosophy and everyday life. hooks asks us to imagine, for example, a group of female students heading to a Women's Studies class hoping for relevant knowledge about the sexual harassment they've faced, only to find the readings so dense, so abstract, that they can't understand them. When and if they do understand the concepts, they don't connect to any "lived realities beyond the classroom. . . . Clearly a feminist theory that can do this may function to legitimize Women's Studies. . . but the purpose of such theory [is] to divide, separate, exclude."[12] In the place of feminist theory here, substitute statistical methods, rhetorical theory, or psychoanalytic approaches to film studies, or any other jargon-filled subarea that might obfuscate meaningful connections for students. Those theories, if taught in a different manner, might have plenty of everyday relevance. Instructors can encourage students to make those connections by sharing their own and creating assignments that facilitate reflection on links between the abstract and the concrete. Done skillfully, "a simple practice like including personal experience may be more constructively challenging than simply changing the curriculum. . .linking that knowledge with academic information really enhances our capacity to know."[13]

Oftentimes the academy values the type of writing that only "a small cadre of people can possibly understand."[14] Although this kind of theoretical work may provide professors with status and publications, even if the ideas are important, these ideas cannot serve to liberate students if they remain inaccessible. Jargon might threaten to overwhelm students' ability to understand key concepts, let alone apply them to the everyday communication phenomena that impact their experiences. Of course, students who first encounter complex ideas and histories will have to work hard, even struggle with materials. However, hooks cautions us to be self-reflexive as we teach difficult subjects so that we do not intentionally or unintentionally fall into dominator mode and act as gatekeepers of knowledge,

---

12. Ibid., 65.
13. Ibid., 148.
14. Katie King, quoted in *Teaching to Transgress*, 64.

screening our students for the "best and brightest" who don't seem to experience difficulties, who learn in the ways we learned.

Performance—an obviously "embodied" form of knowledge—is another way to provide students with alternative paths to theory. Michelle Rassulo and Michael Hecht, for example, used drama to teach issues involving stepfamily communication issues and to challenge participants' understandings and assumptions about families. Their technique, called "trigger scripting," uses performance of scripts "triggered" by academic writing to stimulate discussion. Participants watch the performance before entering into a discussion guided by starter questions. Rassulo and Hecht found that "the performance of literary and narrative texts promotes education and attitude modification" beyond what traditional discussions promoted.[15] Professors and students at Arizona State University continue to use trigger scripting performance and discussion techniques not only in classroom work, but also in public forums dedicated to issues such as immigration and voter ID laws.[16] Interacting with dramatized versions of theory, concepts, and controversies is a form of translational engagement, a way to make clear the theory-practice connection that hooks emphasizes in her work.

Beyond integrating practices that clarify concepts, encourage dialogue and interaction with peers, though, hooks and her colleagues emphasize that students need to practice critical thought, not just to share personal experiences for the sake of sharing. In a conversation with Ron Scrapp, hooks concurs with his observation that sharing personal experiences and listening to them with respect and care does not mean suspending critique. Rather, students and instructors need to "relate experience to the academic subject matter" and keep the conversation focused on the collaborative, dialogic process building toward greater understanding and enriching the learning community.[17] If classroom discussion finds students sharing their multifarious experiences without tethering to history or theory, then students learn only that "we're all different," but not what those differences might do, or from whence they came. Instead, even when things might be uncomfortable as students confront issues of power and inequalities, instructors should strive to create an environment of learning in a community where we can challenge each other without seeking to shame someone, to call for accountability without exacting performances of guilt. In an interview with Buddhist nun Pema Chödrön, hooks asked for an explanation of the difference between blame and accountability. Chödrön answered:

---

15. Rassulo and Hecht, "Performance as Persuasion," 51.
16. Personal communication with Jennifer Linde, Arizona State University. Also see the work of Linde's students in trigger script performance at http://humancommunication.clas.asu.edu/content/empty-space-season-2008-2009 and Linde and John Genette's work on civil dialogue at http://humancommunication.clas.asu.edu/content/civil-dialogue.
17. hooks, *Teaching to Transgress.*, 153.

Accountability seems to mean you can be honest, incredibly honest. You see that harm is being done. You see someone harming a child. . .another human being. You see that clearly and your strongest wish is to de-escalate that suffering. . . . [Y]ou begin to try to find the skillful means to communicate so that the barriers come down rather than get reinforced. It has everything to do with communication: how can you communicate so that someone can hear what you're saying and you can also hear what they are saying?[18]

The goal is not for a partner in dialogue to feel guilt about inequalities, or shame about his or her own privilege within a system built on racial and gender hierarchy; rather, it is to foster a sense of communal resistance to the forces and practices that cause the harm. If through education, for example, we come to see that homophobic stereotypes that circulate on the Internet reinforce a culture of violence against LGBT people, then the point is not to make heterosexual students feel ashamed to be straight and privileged within this system; the goal of critical pedagogy would be to provide them with insights and tools that would demonstrate to them how to be allies of LGBT colleagues; how to speak articulately in public against representational practices and public policies that intensify the harm done to LGBT people; to consider that their humanity and sense of citizenship might be enhanced if they engage in struggle in solidarity rather than shrinking away in silence if they choose to recognize their accountability.

hooks offers Paolo Freire as an exemplar of someone who is open to critical dialogue and accountability. She laments that many feminists write Freire off because his early works contain some sexist language and assumptions. But she notes that this foundational thinker for progressive teaching has not ignored or shrugged off his critics. "In Freire's work. . . there are many responses to [feminist] critiques. . . . I learn from this example, from seeing his willingness to struggle non-defensively in print, naming shortcomings of insight, changes in thought, new critical reflections."[19] Moreover, as a critical reader of his work, she saw—even in the writings done prior to his reflections—the value in his work in terms of how it gave her a means to reconceptualize learning and some language with which to critique dominant forms of teaching structured by colonialism and racism. Her simultaneous dismay with the sexist language did not lead her to throw the baby out with the bathwater, nor did her appreciation of aspects of his work make her silent. Rather, she used her feminist thinking to empower her "to engage in a constructive critique of Freire's work. . .and yet there are many other standpoints from which I approach his work that enable me to experience its value."[20]

18. Interview with Pema Chödrön in *Shambhala Sun*. Accessed from http://www.shambhala.com/html/learn/features/pema/interview/index.cfm
19. hooks, *Teaching to Transgress*, 54–55.
20. Ibid., 49.

Dialogue and careful, critical inclusion of personal narratives are not the only means for implementing liberatory pedagogy, and hooks does not lay out a guidebook with specific plans for transforming classrooms. As Henry Giroux recently wrote,

> Pedagogy is not some recipe that can be imposed on all classrooms. On the contrary, it must always be contextually defined, allowing it to respond specifically to the conditions, formations and problems that arise in various sites in which education takes place. . . . Recognizing this, educators can both address the meaning and purpose that schools might play in their relationship to the demands of the broader society while simultaneously being sensitive to the distinctive nature of the issues educators address within the shifting contexts in which they interact with a diverse body of students, texts and institutional formations.[21]

Being radically present-oriented and willing to change structures and practices as the classroom situation requires is what hooks calls for instructors to consider. For example, she recalls how she had to alter her syllabus and classroom discussions of African American literature when she realized that more and more of her Black students were coming from Caribbean and African communities and didn't share the same historical experiences as her U.S.-born students.

Though some might desire more than just anecdotes, part of hooks' approach is that the challenge of multicultural education is that there are no universal templates for action. A lot of the changes will result from experimentation and flux. Indeed, those who are used to the blueprints of method and theories that guide research may be intimidated or overwhelmed by the openness of critical pedagogy. She recalls that many of her colleagues "found that as they tried to respect 'cultural diversity' they had to confront the limitations of their training, knowledge, and possible loss of 'authority.' Indeed, exploring certain truths and biases in the classroom often created chaos and confusion" and upended the notion of "safe" or predictable curricular plans.[22] When the biases and frictions over truth come to the fore, it is imperative, in hooks' philosophy, to keep an eye on the values and goals of liberatory education so as not to lapse into fear or cynicism. If the main goal is to "decolonize our minds," then we have to be ready for struggle, for discomfort and ambiguity, as we incorporate new materials and cultural approaches to re-think questions of knowledge, power, freedom, and identity.

Content Matters: Decolonizing the Canon

Many of the "culture wars" debates are centered on the notion of disciplinary canons. Critics of multicultural education warn of a time when the "Great Books"

---

21. Giroux, "Dangerous Pedagogy in the Age of Casino Capitalism."
22. hooks, "A Revolution of Values."

(classics written by a group of mostly European and white American male scholars) would be totally eradicated from university classrooms, replaced by contemporary works by (in their minds) inferior scholars of color, feminists, and so forth, under the banner of "political correctness." This caricature of multiculturalism posits that the project of inclusion is essentially opposed to merit and that the goal is to replace the hegemony of one group with that of another. Many of the pundits and critics of multiculturalism (mostly on the Right) would have us believe that this reversal of hegemony has already taken place, and that neither white male scholarship nor white male professors can be easily found on "liberal" campuses.[23] This hysteria is unfounded, and it misses the central point of diversifying higher education. For hooks and her comrades in progressive education, the process of questioning the canon is never about the simple displacement of one group in favor of others. It is about *how* to teach and *whom* we teach as much as it is about what we should teach and who does the teaching, and understanding how these elements are intertwined. When we begin to re-examine one component, we must address the others.

Once we see that the materials and modes of teaching prescribed in the dominant pedagogical and canonical paradigms were based in large part on who had access to learning and the power to bestow the "Great Books" designation on particular texts, then we can see it would be ineffective merely to swap titles in the libraries. Dismantling the dominant educational paradigms that restricted knowledge creation and dissemination requires us to take a multifaceted approach to including new elements in the curriculum. In short, content matters, but the transformation of content should happen in concert with other progressive changes.

New Wine in Old Bottles? The Problems of Tokenism and Colorblindness

Many critical scholars have deconstructed the notion of a universal canon of great works and theories that transcend culture, space, and time. I will not spend much time here rehearsing their arguments—readers can seek their extended critiques elsewhere.[24] Once we recognize how "the canon" is actually a historically and politically situated list of scholarly or artistic works—whether it be The Great Books of Feminist Philosophy or Communication Theory—we can be open to understanding the need to be wary of the processes of selection that drive the formation of canons, and attend to how systemic discrimination and limited access to scholarly institutions have shaped the "classic" lists of Great Thinkers and Literature. Acknowledging that canons are not objective is part of recognizing that "the privileged act of naming often affords those in power access to modes

---

23. hooks, *Teaching Community*, 85.
24. See, for example, Kahaney and Liu, eds., *Contested Terrain: Diversity, Writing & Knowledge;* Pierce-Baker, "A Quilting of Voices."

of communication and enables them to project an interpretation, a definition, a description of their work and actions, that may not be accurate, that may obscure what is really taking place."[25]

When works are named to the canon, the interpretive and subjective acts of those empowered to decide what is Literature or Art are often obscured behind discourses of objectivity, merit, and so forth. Recognizing this is not a reason to trash a canon or the notion that we can discern greatness in a given discipline; rather, once the myth of objectivity is dismantled, scholars and students can experience canonical works anew. This way, the process of broadening, editing, or reconsidering the canon becomes a transparent and potentially liberating enterprise where we can situate knowledge and share across domains of experience and history.

This process suggests that dissecting and reconstituting the basic curriculum in a field requires us to do much more than reshuffle the authors on our reading lists, taking care to include people from different cultures and nations in the films, books, or articles we consume. If we recognize the operation of power, culture, and history in the formation of curricula, then as we try to shed dominator modes of teaching and learning that exclude Others, we must take care not to pour the new wine into old bottles. If we deliver the new content in the same manner as the old—pretending that race or gender or language doesn't matter—then the richness of multicultural learning won't necessarily come through. hooks illustrates the problem by asking,

> What does it mean when a white female English teacher is eager to include a work by Toni Morrison. . . but then teaches that work without ever making reference to race or ethnicity?. . . Clearly such pedagogy is not an interrogation of the biases conventional canons (if not all canons) establish, but yet another form of tokenism.[26]

Of course it is important to teach Morrison's work to students in ways that recognize her debt to Modernism, to the formal stylizations and influence of writers such as Faulkner. But Morrison's genius and contributions lie not only in those strands of literary form, but also in her dedication to excavating and explicating black experiences in America in ways that attend to specific legacies of slavery and racism. How she writes about the experiences of pain, ecstasy and agony, love and recovery in her books matters because she conveys black experiences in a way no one has before. Indeed, in her own writings she is explicit about creating black literature, writing about race-specific issues, but in ways that can speak to any audience. An instructor need not choose between teaching the form of her work or the import of its content; rather, she can show how Morrison illuminates our understanding of universal human desires, needs, faults through the specific

---

25. hooks, *Teaching to Transgress*, 62.
26. Ibid., 38–39.

experiences of black characters, just as Homer communicates our understanding of the bonds of soldiers and human costs of war in his telling of the impact of war on ancient Greek men and women in the *Iliad* and the *Odyssey*. Like Morrison, Homer's works are bound by cultural and formal elements, poetic structures, and knowledge of historical events. If teachers don't explain how and why the specificities inform the generalities, and open up new ways to think about core ideas and values, then including people of color or women or gays or differently abled folks in a new canon merely pays lip service to diversity, and opportunities to expand learning are lost.

This discussion suggests that we need to take care with how we add to the canon. If we single out only one "Other" writer, such as Morrison, and she continues to be the only Other on the syllabus, it suggests that she's there to "liven up" the curriculum, to stand in for "a different perspective," thereby reinforcing the unstated notion that white male writers provide normative, universal perspectives in literature. To bring in only one or two non-dominant representatives implies that there are too few to create a more diverse syllabus, or that there are not enough excellent examples from that Other group to merit inclusion with the Great Books. Without a broader consideration of why we should diversify the canon and how to teach a more diverse set of works than we are used to, students may get the wrong idea about inclusion, or become frustrated at the paltry selection. This will leave many with the idea that tokenism is all that is possible, or assume that there are still insufficient numbers of women of color or gay men to fill out a course. As teachers, we need to better serve students who are cognizant of the "culture wars" and may be caught in the crossfire as they explore their own identities and interact with people of different backgrounds.

Diverse Canons for Diverse Classrooms

Coming at the issue of canons from the perspective of serving our students, then, it is fairly easy to argue that a diverse store of content will better "match" a more diverse student body. To a certain extent, this conjecture is reasonable: the symbolic annihilation of marginalized peoples in academia or media is a problem that requires remedy. It is a shock to the systems of students from underrepresented groups to find that supposedly "multicultural" colleges don't actually present students with a robust range of scholarly, cultural, and historical resources. Replicating the underrepresentation (or misrepresentations) of the media or government presents a less-than-welcoming environment and reinforces the sense that such students and their communities are not worthy unless they assimilate. Indeed, hooks wrote *Ain't I a Woman* in part to combat the exclusion and absence of women of color from English and Women's Studies. As she wrote in *Talking Back*, when white feminist editors questioned the tone of *Ain't I a Woman*—telling her it didn't sound like it was "for them"—she replied that she wrote it for Black women, the women whose experiences and histories were not yet represented in feminist literature. She wrote it, in part, as a response to the frustrations and silencing she felt as she navigated college and graduate school. Hegemonic thought cannot be challenged effectively if gatekeepers allow only marginal voices a hearing if "what is said [is] overdetermined by the needs of that majority group who appears to be listening. . . in a language compatible with existing images and ways of knowing."[27] So professors—who act as editors for their students—must reflect on their assumptions about audiences and expectations for "satisfying" those audiences when evaluating the contributions of students from marginalized groups.

At the same time, it is not welcoming to students to put them in a box labeled with their ethnicity or sexuality. That is, when teaching material about Black women writers, instructors should not expect black female students to be "experts" or lead discussions as some sort of "native informant" for others who don't share the identity of the authors. This is essentialism at its worst, suggesting that all black people share special knowledge and affinity for black-authored works and that the main role and responsibility for students of color on campus is to translate Other work for white students and instructors. It reinforces the same asymmetric relations of power and knowledge that allow white people to act as if they don't have to confront the issues of race from their experience as members of the dominant group, but only vicariously through the experiences of subordinate groups. This does not mean that there isn't sometimes more overlap in experiences or historical knowledge for people who share an ascribed identity; it does mean that instructors can't make the assumption that this overlap exists or is relevant to any particular student, or that she or he would feel comfortable voicing that affinity. Moreover, if professors turn only to students of color when a race-matched author is the topic of discussion, the student may feel pigeonholed, or valued as a learner in a narrow role.[28]

This pigeonholing and essentialism can affect how people respond to the student's work or voice. hooks relates how essentialist understandings of an "authentic voice" can warp instructors' perceptions of how female students or students of color should write or speak. In *Talking Back*, she recalls how her English professor only praised her work as "authentic" when she used Black vernacular, but not when she used Standard English. Here, we see how stereotypes can hinder expression. hooks rejected the definition of authentic voice—and the premise that "finding one voice, one definitive style of writing and reading one's poetry" was more authentic than exploring different styles and techniques. The professor's notion of authenticity reinforced a "static notion of self and identity."[29] Elsewhere,

---

27. hooks, *Talking Back*, 14.
28. TuSmith and Reddy, *Race in the College Classroom*; Chesler, "Perceptions of Faculty Behavior."
29. hooks, *Talking Back*, 11.

she reflects on how she found joy and self-esteem through recitation exercises at her school, where she and her classmates might memorize a poem by Phyllis Wheatley or William Shakespeare in a given session, and be called on to perform either, without a sense that speaking the words of the Black poetess was more "authentic" than articulating the stanzas of the White bard. Forcing someone to see one mode of expression as "authentic" because it matches racial identities of author and reader does not affirm the values of multiculturalism; it squelches them.

Thus, changing the content of our courses must always be done in consideration of and in response to who is in the classroom. hooks notes that once a professor masters a content area, such as Black literature, she can't rest on her laurels and repeat the same lesson plans year after year, class after class. If the original syllabus was crafted when the students enrolled were, say, African American and white American, expectations for knowledge of U.S. history and experiences with systems of racial identification would suggest particular approaches to the works of Alice Walker. But what if the class is now made up of more foreign-born students, or students who came of age well after the civil rights movement? hooks offers herself as an example, reflecting on the need to continually recognize the shifting diversity of her students "to recognize what I have called in other writings 'cultural codes.' To teach effectively a diverse student body, I have to learn these codes. And so do students."[30] Learning cultural codes requires a commitment to listening and sharing the desire to learn from one another.

If one of the major aspirations of multicultural education is to provide students with experiences that will enhance their ability to learn, live, and work with people of different backgrounds, then we can't just throw them in the classrooms together and draw solely upon pedagogies that were structured by exclusion and assumptions of homogeneity. If another aspiration of multicultural education is to have students engage in critical thought to deconstruct common myths and stereotypes about Others, then we can't just include new works in "the canon" and hope they figure it out without mentioning anything about difference. hooks advises instructors to include diverse works in ways that invite and challenge all of us "to shift paradigms rather than to appropriate, to have all readers listen" to previously excluded voices and hear them as subjects, "not as underprivileged other."[31] The canon positioned white males as universal subjects and everyone else as lesser objects. The real test of multicultural education's revision of the canon is in how students and instructors undo that equation so that the humanity of marginalized peoples is made plain, accessible, and transformative. This task requires us to reimagine who, where, and how to educate people within and outside the academy.

---

30. hooks, *Teaching to Transgress*, 41.
31. hooks, *Talking Back*, 16.

Education as Liberation: Forging New Habits of Mind Through Criticism

hooks teaches cultural criticism within a pedagogy that is "fundamentally linked to a concern with creating strategies that will enable colonized folks to decolonize their minds and actions."[32] She is concerned that much feminist and other critical work is being confined to university classrooms. She suggests that students and teachers take the tools learned in democratic classrooms into other spaces that are more accessible. Sharing these liberatory resources "in small group contexts, integrating critical analysis with discussion of personal experience," would increase the spaces where people learned how to engage in "dialectical struggle."[33] In these dialogues, people forge bonds and elevate their consciousness, even when conversations about race, power, gender, and other axes of difference are difficult to sustain. "Fear of painful confrontation often leads women and men. . .to avoid rigorous critical encounter, yet if we cannot engage dialectically in a committed, rigorous, humanizing manner, we cannot hope to change the world."[34] Because critical, liberatory education is about deconstructing dominator culture and imagining different ways of relating to each other, oftentimes critical dialogues involve imagining, opening "ourselves to the unknown" and not getting to consensus in one sitting.[35] To this end, hooks calls upon educators and activists to record and share their accounts of the ways people have successfully confronted differences in a constructive, successful way, and to share "detailed accounts of the ways our lives are fuller and richer as we change and grow politically. . .as comrades."[36] This kind of sharing not only facilitates the growth and reach of constructive engagement between diverse peoples, but also reminds us that there can be joy, love, and care in struggles for equality and that when we work so that all people can live up to their potential, we make ourselves—not just others—more free.

Many people do not have access to the kinds of training that make it easier to transition into the conventions and quirks of academic writing, to decode and translate "high theory." hooks finds it terribly ironic that many theorists of postmodernism, cultural studies, and feminism—bodies of thought that emerged from radical movements and critiques of the status quo—are content to publish their work in exclusive journals and give talks to specialized audiences. In this vein, she calls for folks to be more open to working outside the academy, to publish widely, to seek and meet different audiences. Again, hooks uses her own experiences reaching out to diverse audiences, and the proof of their reactions—and understanding her conveyance of theory/praxis—to debunk "the prevailing notion that it is simply too difficult to make connections" with people outside

32. hooks, *Yearning*, 8.
33. hooks, *Talking Back*, 24.
34. Ibid., 25.
35. Ibid.
36. Ibid., 26

college classrooms or academic presses.[37] Moreover, she sees this as integral to the postmodern critiques of power, knowledge, and agency.

hooks teaches cultural criticism within a pedagogy that is "fundamentally linked to a concern with creating strategies that will enable colonized folks to decolonize their minds and actions."[38] She calls on teachers to cultivate "habits of being that reinforce awareness that knowledge can be disseminated and shared on a number of fronts. The extent to which knowledge is made available, accessible, etc., depends on the nature of one's political commitments."[39] To her, this means that postmodernist theory isn't just about rupture and deconstruction, but also about creating new spaces and practices, for in the gaps created by ruptures we might "make space for oppositional practices which no longer require intellectuals to be confined by narrow separate spheres with no meaningful connection to the world of the everyday."[40] This is another reason why using pop culture in the classroom—and making it an object of analysis—is vital: popular culture becomes "a meeting place where new and radical happenings can occur" with the participation of artists, intellectuals, and everyday people.[41]

Critical Pedagogy, Media, and Democracy

The passive model of student learning isn't only problematic in terms of the classroom dynamics it generates; hooks sees a link to students' diminished ability to engage meaningfully in critical, political discourse beyond the university. In this way, her work resonates with Rosa Eberly's conceptualization of classrooms as "proto-public spheres." Building from Habermas' understanding of literary publics as precursors to discussions of politics policy, Eberly, like hooks, calls on educators to recognize the need to revive publicly engaged criticism. Learning literary criticism not just in terms of the formal attributes of texts, but also in terms of how they relate to contemporary controversies and topics, can provide students with opportunities to "manifest a public-oriented subjectivity, that is, a self that is more or less able to turn private reactions about literary or cultural texts into discourses that address some shared concerns."[42] For hooks, popular films and television provide ideal vehicles for engagement with theory and cultivating the sociological imagination.

> I began to realize that my students learned more about race, sex, and class from movies than from all the theoretical literature I was urging them to read. . . .

37. hooks, *Teaching Community*, x.
38. Ibid., 8.
39. Ibid., 30–31.
40. Ibid., 31.
41. Ibid.
42. Eberly, *Citizen Critics: Literary Public Spheres*, 9.

Movies. . .provide a shared experience, a common starting point from which
diverse audiences can dialogue about these charged issues.[43]

hooks' response to the other oft-recited truism in Communication Studies—
that media are ubiquitous in the contemporary world—is that we should use
media as a teaching tool. Discussing media and teaching critical skills—not just
tearing down a media text or author, but clearly analyzing its connections to history, culture, power—are not just classroom exercises, but exercises in liberating
one's mind. Dissecting how a film draws upon and extends a notorious stereotype
about black masculinity, for example, not only teaches skills of deconstruction,
but also opens up space for students to talk about race in a profound manner.
Popular films, then, can be useful, often powerful, pedagogical tools for engaging with social issues and theories simultaneously. Students can learn to be critics
who recognize that movies "offer us the opportunity to reimagine the culture we
most intimately know on screen" and to interrogate cinema's power to "create new
awareness, to transform culture" and/or to reinforce the dominant norms of that
culture.[44]

hooks provides many stories about breakthroughs in her classes, and some
communication scholars influenced by her writings and other critical media literacy work have systematically studied the impact of film on their students. In
one of the few studies to evaluate what students are learning from diversity-in-
media courses, Tina Harris concluded that instructors should use a variety of
pedagogical tools—films, readings, discussion—to be more successful in relating
the materials to students and to advance their critical thinking skills. In particular,
the films Harris showed generated an emotional response and helped to clarify
the concept of race for many of her students.[45] Still, some white students felt
a distance and weren't able to sympathize with experiences of discrimination.[46]
Similar to Harris, Dwight Brooks and Christa Ward found that films provided
opportunities for students to relate to situations involving race, helped students
grasp more concepts, and increased classroom engagement. As the class increasingly discussed white privilege, students acknowledged whiteness with greater
ease. However, most students still struggled to connect white privilege to racism and discrimination: "although some acknowledged the invisible taken-for-
granted nature of whiteness few wanted to identify or discuss the privileges being
white and male bestows."[47] Although some students were apprehensive, Brooks
and Ward concluded in-class videos were beneficial to students and effective in
engaging students with concepts and terms.

43. hooks, *Reel to Real*, 3.
44. Ibid., 12.
45. Harris, "Student Reactions to Visual Texts."
46. Harris, 114.
47. Brooks and Ward, "Assessing Students' Engagement with Pedagogies of Diversity," 251.

While films provide a different, dynamic entry point for students to engage with racial experiences they may not have had in their own lives, some students do not respond well to diverse curricular offerings. Julia Johnson, Mark Rich, and Aaron Cargile's analysis of white students' journal entries revealed very aggressive, angry responses to diversity curriculum. The researchers collected and coded student journals from intercultural courses offered at two different universities over the span of three years. Four main themes emerged in white students' journals: (1) acknowledgment of racism; (2) white self-preservation; (3) diversion from structural power; and (4) investment in white supremacy. Often these white students were angry that people of color complained about racism. For example, one student journal entry said "they [blacks] should be happy that America freed them 'cuz now they are free."[48] Other students felt guilt for white privilege but did not believe the system could change. Margaret Hunter and Kimberly Nettles' white students resisted engagement with works authored by women of color and felt they were not being represented.[49] Likewise, Jennifer Trainor found similar issues of overt racism as well as denial and guilt amongst white students when discussing race.[50] Clearly, the variety of reactions and levels of engagement with materials suggest that there are no foolproof methods of addressing racial issues in the classroom. However, some are more successful than others. Longer-term, focused engagements that allow for discussion seem to reap great benefits beyond the classroom. While not focused on media studies per se, research from a seven-university study shows that students who took courses that required them to work in diverse teams and/or discussion groups while they engaged with the diversity curriculum resulted in more diverse post-graduate living and working experiences.[51]

> *Animated by a sense of critique and possibility, critical pedagogy at its best attempts to provoke students to deliberate, resist and cultivate a range of capacities that enable them to move beyond the world they already know without insisting on a fixed set of meanings.*[52]
> —Henry Giroux

Practicing habits of mind that foster dialogue and critical thought about media is key in a society saturated with images and narratives of identity, power, and belonging. Moreover, if people are not able to learn and try out different ways of seeing and thinking within a community, then the problem of underrepresentation of critical voices in the public sphere will continue to undermine progressive change. Recall hooks' dismay at the lack of variety and depth of criticism in

---

48. Johnson, Rich, and Castelan Cargile. "'Why Are You Shoving This Stuff Down Our Throats?'" 113.
49. Hunter and Nettles, "What About White Women?"
50. Trainor, "My Ancestors Didn't Own Slaves."
51. Gurin, Nagda, and Lopez. "The Benefits of Diversity in Education."
52. Giroux, "Dangerous Pedagogy."

circulation about the rising number of black films.[53] She aims to provide learning experiences with media that will inspire at least some of them to move from private spectator to public speaker, to make the classroom, as Eberly puts it, "a *locus* for inventing public-oriented subjectivities, something increasingly difficult to understand and do as public life is continually eroded."[54] hooks means it when she titles a book "Teaching Community": too many people, socialized within a dominator culture that values individualism over community, do not learn about the spectrum of ways to interact with their fellow citizens. Dominant neoliberal discourses devalue the notion that the public is worth recuperating, making it imperative for alternative spaces to incubate public-oriented practices.

Even though film criticism is largely dominated by people who do not share her approach to analyzing the role of race, class, and gender, hooks does not "despair, because I see the power of progressive cultural criticism in the classroom setting and recognize that location as a crucial site for critical intervention."[55] Some of her students express how they feel like they can't just enjoy media—or life!—after taking her classes. As one group told her, "We learn to look at the world from a critical standpoint, one that considers race, sex and class. And we can't enjoy life anymore."[56] But she tries to convince them that there is excitement and joy to be had in making critical statements, and to have compassion for themselves and their colleagues as they experience the "pain involved in giving up old ways of thinking and knowing and learning new approaches. . . . I include recognition of it now when I teach."[57] Providing opportunities to reflect on these feelings is important: making room to acknowledge the emotional, intimate components of critical thinking. Instructors have to know that deep discussions of racism and social struggles may make some white students, for example, "suddenly see their parents in a different light,"[58] or make students of color feel doomed to "disrupt feelings of racial bonding and solidarity" if they turn a critical eye on a black filmmaker's work.[59] Rather, they should welcome the opportunity to have a richer, deeper, perhaps more constructive discussion, which will hopefully strengthen the basis for inter- or intra-racial solidarity by providing a clearer view of the multiple perspectives necessary to engender cultural transformation. Students and scholars can only engage in critical dialogue that sustains rather than breaks bonds if they learn how to "distinguish between hostile critique that is about 'trashing' and critique that's about illuminating and enriching our understanding" of a film or

---

53. e.g., hooks, *Yearning*, 2–3; *Black Looks*, 6–7.
54. Eberly, *Citizen Critics*, 10.
55. hooks, *Yearning*, 6.
56. hooks, *Teaching to Transgress*, 42.
57. Ibid., 43.
58. Ibid.
59. hooks, *Yearning*, 6.

song or video.[60] Getting students to go beyond a positive/negative diagnosis and to practice reflection and listening is how classrooms build community.

Educational institutions need to make room for students and teachers to learn holistically, to integrate experiences and make space for transformation. Media can provide inroads for the kind of dialogue and interaction hooks envisions. In the example provided above, students were able to begin on common ground through the film they'd all seen, all experienced. From there, the film became a medium for discussion of larger issues that were thematized, allowing the students to connect and reflect on their own experiences of race, gender, class. Here we see the encouragement of an intersectional sociological imagination: the students are practicing how to connect the personal to the social, to the political. They can begin to see how their consciousness has been shaped so that they are not expected to question the validity of the "realistic" images presented by movies, how their schooling, neighborhood locations, and so on, have separated them from people represented on the screen, so that all they think they "know" about "real people" is actually manufactured by an industry that aims not to promote social integration or anti-racism, but to generate profits. Sharing stories of her classroom in this ethnographic manner, hooks provides us with an intimate view of how media literacy has the potential to reframe discussions of politics, to give students and everyday people a more accessible inroad to theories of media and politics. This is theory connected to practice, theory connected to experience, to real life, in a visceral way.

---

60. Ibid., 7.

epilogue

Notes on Revisiting
Critical Theorist bell hooks

One way to consider the scope of bell hooks' career is to think of her as constantly exploring the tensions and connections between personal and political, reality and image. From her first book, *Ain't I a Woman*, written in part to respond to the stark absence of black women in the academy, to recent works such as *Salvation*, written to urge people to heal the wounds of dominator culture, hooks searches for multiple ways to convey dialectical relationships between self and society. Between *Black Looks* and *We Real Cool*, she articulates the relations between self and media, reality and fiction, art and life. While some might ask her to focus her attention squarely on particular, fixed objects of inquiry in line with traditional research practices, as a cultural critic she has illuminated for us key questions to be asked and asked again as the media landscape changes. This book, I hope, has clarified some of hooks' theoretical approaches and suggested how her understanding of power and justice can inform all aspects of academic practice.

Surveying her most influential work, it is clear that her investments in intersectionality, anti-essentialism, and the presence of power in all situations, benefit our investigations of media at many levels. Looking to the work that has drawn criticism of late, we can still learn from her example as a thinker who pushes ideas to be publicly relevant, to meet people where they are. While I do agree with some of her critics that the books framed as self-help (such as *Remembered Rapture* and *All About Love*) fall short of the practical wisdom promised in the introductory pages, we can learn from her mistakes. Rather than engage in "tearing down" type criticism, we should ask of these texts: where could we integrate more solid examples and research results? How might we provide more grounded, tested examples of the practices necessary to change homeplaces, classrooms, or public spaces? If we follow hooks' call to make our work publicly relevant, to contest the divisions between academic and popular writing, then we can learn as much from her successes in translating theory into practice as we can from her less successful forays. Relatedly, as scholars in the social sciences and humanities are challenged by government, industry, students, and funders to justify the relevance of our curricula and research endeavors, what can we learn from hooks that might give us some clues for articulating our defense? Or better, what examples does she provide for demonstrating our contributions to our society's well-being?

Scholars in Communication Studies, I suggest, should be particularly keen to draw upon hooks' demonstrations of how to put theory into practice. Given the hyper-interpenetration of media into all realms of life—screens and signals can accompany our every move—communication researchers and teachers can leverage the best of her understandings of media, representation, and democracy to craft applied research projects as well as theoretical explorations of how group and individual identity, sense of agency, and sense of community are changing in our ever-expanding mediascapes. How are "old" ways of relating to "Others" migrating online, for instance? Some recent research suggests that people continue to employ race, gender, and class biases cultivated off-line when they surf the Internet. Studies have found that: female bloggers are rated less expert than male bloggers; social media enthusiasts have racialized MySpace as the social network for people of color, Facebook as the white social network; and that the relative anonymity of the Net inspires the most putrid expressions of homophobia.[1] For every "It Gets Better" campaign that leverages the Internet to push against hateful renderings of marginalized groups, there are websites with all the "old-style" racism, sexism, and classism found in "old media." Taking off from her critiques of the expanding opportunities for black representation in media, one might ask: Are the opportunities afforded in cyberspace really breaking new ground, and if so, in what ways?

Similarly, hooks' discussions of media, power, and racial representation in the postmodern age prompt the question: Are celebrations of technological advancement or access displacing arguments about social justice in the same way that excitement over postmodernism and "choice" suggested no need for collective identities as a basis for collective action? Just as Black and Latino youth devel-

---

1. See chapters in *Race After the Internet*, Nakamura and Chow White, eds., for research on racial profiling and usage on MySpace vs. Facebook. See also discussions of gender, sexuality, and hate speech online in essays such as: Armstrong and McAdams, "Believing Blogs"; Rogers, "Video Game Design and Acceptance of Hate Speech"; and Cooper, "Anti-Gay Speech on the Internet," all in Lind, ed., *Race/Gender/Class/Media*.

oped hip hop to carve out voice and space in public spheres, many postmodernist scholars leveraged anti-essentialist arguments to deny the validity of using group identity to spark any political practices. hooks pushed back, wondering whether these specific renderings of anti-essentialism amounted to a "dismissal of the struggle of oppressed and exploited people to make ourselves subjects," and asked her colleagues to take more care to differentiate between vulgar racial essentialism and recognition of how "black identity has been specifically constituted in the experience of . . . struggle."[2] Although she agreed that theorizing politics from the experiences shared rather than skin color made more sense, it is hard to separate the experiences from the imposed classifications that delineate marginal status.

Discussions of the "freedoms" and "access" to media "choices" in the marketplace often assume the menu of options is culturally diverse enough for everyone and that all barriers to equal opportunity have been vanquished. But, as discussed in Chapter Five, audiences/consumers are neither valued equally nor are they equally served by dominant media. Thus, we must remain skeptical when people claim there is no necessity for protests about representation or regulation of mass media. When we assess the range of choices, we need to be careful to contextualize our investigation and attend to who has the most choices and what that range of choice will facilitate in terms of resource allocation and political empowerment. We should likewise push back on those who rhapsodize about the wide range of choices available via a technologically sophisticated media marketplace without accounting for the continued patterns of discrimination and limited access for people of color as well as problematic gendered roles and hierarchies.

As we continue to interrogate the limits and opportunities of the global media landscape and its ever-changing technical capacities, we should also have hooks and her feminist cultural studies colleagues' questions echoing in our minds. Whose standpoints dominate the way we frame our research questions? Who stands to benefit most from allowing these normalized standpoints to seem "neutral"? Have we considered whether the habits of mind and practices we are encouraged to engage in online are merely high tech, digitized versions of the dominator culture mindsets we hoped to leave behind in the analogue world?

When we teach the great works in our field, do we reify the contributions of a handful of the same scholars, or do we dig deeper to understand who might have been left out of the pantheon and why? Central to hooks' project is situating knowledge in everyday life, to decrease the often-intimidating distance between scholars and the lay public—particularly marginalized groups. This is not done to satisfy a missionary desire to "save the people," but rather to challenge and unravel the hierarchies that academia exists within and, at times, perpetuates through unwritten codes of engagement and exchange. In this vein, hooks presents her own

---

2. hooks, *Yearning*, 29.

life experiences with education and cultural consumption as spaces of resistance and pleasure and calls on readers to question why or why not their academic experiences or workplaces do not foster counter hegemonic thought or provide pleasurable, nurturing interactions.

To close, I suggest that we might profit most from appreciating and learning from hooks ways to be critical scholars. As Kent Ono wrote, not all scholarship is critical; that which is critical attends to questions of power and pauses to "discuss what is at stake" as we look in new directions to push the field.[3] bell hooks urges us to remain vibrantly critical as we pursue whatever research paths, teaching philosophies, or public speaking opportunities make up our contributions to our field. Reviewing her substantial body of work provides us with time to pause, to discuss, to think about the potential of our work to impact the lives of our students, our colleagues, and people beyond the walls of academia.

I was reminded to pause very recently, as I taught one of the last sessions of my class on race, gender, and media. Over the course of a week, an avalanche of news stories that implicated hooks' work roared into view: the tragic, possibly racially motivated, shooting of a young African American man; the passage of yet another anti-gay marriage law; congressional hearings aimed at restricting women's access to gynecological health services that had any link to contraception. I interwove a comment about one of these issues into a lecture, and a young woman in the middle row raised her hand to ask me, "Professor Squires, can you speak more to that?" Her classmates were nodding in assent: they wanted to pause, not to move on to the next topic, the next reading. Media and race and gender were happening to them in the now, and I had a decision to make. I took a deep breath, and invited my students to begin talking to each other, one on one, about what they already knew; what they *thought* they knew; and what they felt had been left out of the story, what they wanted to know. It was probably one of the best days in class, and it spurred on amazing final papers and projects, and encouraged some students to take part in teach-ins and marches elsewhere. bell hooks' devotion to listening, to pausing, to being critical, can provide us with more ways to engage our field in everyday practices. I hope this book provides many reasons to pause, to reflect, and to move forward in Communication Studies work with a richer understanding of its connections to other people and struggles that perhaps did not seem relevant before.

---

3. Ono, "Critical: A Finer Edge," 96.

Bibliography

Adachi, Jeff. Director, *The Slanted Screen: Asian Men in Film and Television*. San Francisco: Asian American Media Mafia Productions (DVD and VHS) 2006.

Allen, Richard. *The Concept of Self: A Study of Black Identity*. Detroit: Wayne State University Press, 2001.

Ang, Ien. *Living Room Wars: Rethinking Audiences for a Postmodern World*. New York: Routledge, 1996.

Appiah, Kwame Anthony. *Cosmopolitanism: Ethics in a World of Strangers*. New York: W.W. Norton, 2006.

Asen, Robert, and Brower, Daniel, eds. *Counterpublics and the State*. Albany: SUNY Press, 2001.

Beck, Martha. "Four Steps to Aha! How to Figure Out the Life You Want." *O, The Oprah Magazine*, January 2012, 37–39.

Berry, Venise T., and Manning-Miller, Carmen, eds. *Mediated Messages and African-American Culture: Contemporary Issues*. Thousand Oaks: Sage, 1996.

Black Public Sphere Collective, The, eds. *The Black Public Sphere*. Chicago: University of Chicago Press, 1995.

Bobo, Jacqueline. *Black Women As Cultural Readers*. New York: Columbia University Press, 1995.

Brooks, Dwight, and Ward, C. J. "Assessing Students' Engagement with Pedagogies of Diversity." *Journalism and Mass Communication Educator, 62* (2007): 251.

Busselle, Rick, and Crandall, Heather. "Television Viewing and Perceptions About Race Differences in Socioeconomic Success." *Journal of Broadcasting and Electronic Media, 46,* no. 2 (2002): 265–282.

Carter, Prudence L. *Keepin' It Real: School Success Beyond Black and White*. New York: Oxford University Press, 2005.

Chesler, Mark A. "Perceptions of Faculty Behavior by Students of Color." *CRLT Occasional Papers 7* (1997), available at www.crlt.umich.edu/publinks/occasional.php

Dash, Julie. *Daughters of the Dust: The Making of an African American Woman's Film*. New York: New Press, 1992.

Dewey, John. *The Public and Its Problems*. Athens: Ohio University Press, 1954.

Dillard, Angela. *Guess Who's Coming to Dinner Now? Multicultural Conservatism in America*. New York: New York University Press, 2001.

Dixon, Travis, and Azocar, Cristina L. "Priming Crime and Activating Blackness: Understanding the Psychological Impact of the Overrepresentation of Blacks as Lawbreakers on Television News." *Journal of Communication, 57* (2007): 229–253.

Donovan, Roxane A. "Tough or Tender: (Dis)similarities in White College Students' Perceptions of Black and White Women." *Psychology of Women Quarterly, 35,* no. 3 (2011): 458–468.

Eberly, Rosa. *Citizen Critics: Literary Public Spheres*. Champaign-Urbana: University of Illinois Press, 2000.

Entman, Robert M., and Rojecki, Andrew. *The Black Image in the White Mind: Media and Race in America*. Chicago: University of Chicago Press, 2000.

Everett, Anna. *Returning the Gaze: A Genealogy of Black Film Criticism, 1909–1949*. Durham: Duke University Press, 1996.

Faludi, Susan. *Backlash: The Undeclared War Against American Women*. New York: Crown, 1991.

Fisherkeller, JoAnne. "It's Just Like Teaching People to 'Do the Right Things'" in *Say It Loud!*, edited by Robin R. Means Coleman, 147–85. New York: Routledge, 2002.

Fraser, Nancy. "Rethinking the Public Sphere: A Contribution to the Critique of Actually-Existing Democracy." In *Habermas and the Public Sphere*, edited by Craig Calhoun, 109–142, Cambridge: MIT Press, 1992.

Gan, Su-Lin, Zillmann, Dolf, and Mitrook, Michael. "Stereotyping Effect of Black Women's Sexual Rap on White Audiences." *Basic and Applied Social Psychology, 19,* no. 3 (1997): 381–99.

Gandy, Oscar. "Matrix Multiplication and the Digital Divide," in *Race After the Internet*, edited by Lisa Nakamura and Peter Chow-White, 128–145. New York: Routledge, 2012.

George, Nelson. *Buppies. B-boys, Baps and Bohos: Notes on Post-soul Black Culture*. Cambridge: Perseus Press/DaCapo Books, 2001.

Gilroy, Paul. *Against Race: Imagining Political Culture Beyond the Color Line*. Cambridge: Belknap/Harvard University Press, 2000.

Giroux, Henry. "Dangerous Pedagogy in the Age of Casino Capitalism and Religious Fundamentalism." Available at http://www.truth-out.org/dangerous-pedagogy-age-casino-capitalism-and-religious-fundamentalism/1330459170

Gunn, Joshua, and Cloud, Dana. "Agentic Orientation as Magical Voluntarism," *Communication Theory, 20* (2010): 50–79.

Gurin, Patricia, Nagda, Birin, and Lopez, Gretchen. "The Benefits of Diversity in Education for Democratic Citizenship." *Journal of Social Issues, 60* (2004): 17–34.

Habermas, Jürgen. *The Structural Transformation of the Public Sphere: An Inquiry into a Category of Bourgeois Society*. Translated by Thomas Burger. Cambridge: MIT Press, 1989.

Harris, Tina. "Student Reactions to the Visual Texts the Color of Fear and Rosewood in the Interracial Classroom." *The Howard Journal of Communication, 12* (April 2001): 101–117.

Herbst, Susan. *Rude Democracy: Civility & Incivility in American Politics*. Philadelphia: Temple University Press, 2010.

Hill Collins, Patricia. *Black Feminist Thought: Knowledge, Consciousness, and the Politics of Empowerment*. New York: Routledge, 1991.

hooks, bell. *Ain't I a Woman? Black Women and Feminism*. Boston: South End Press Collective, 1981.

——. *Talking Back: Thinking Feminist, Thinking Black*. Boston: South End Press, 1989.

——. *Black Looks: Race and Representation*. Boston: South End Press, 1992.

——. *Outlaw Culture: Resisting Representations*. New York: Routledge, 1994.

——. *Teaching to Transgress: Education As the Practice of Freedom*. New York: Routledge, 1994.

——. *Killing Rage, Ending Racism*. New York: Henry Holt, 1995.

——. *Bone Black: Memories of Girlhood*. New York: Henry Holt, 1996.

——. *Reel to Real: Race, Sex & Class at the Movies*. New York: Routledge, 1996.

——. *Yearning: Race, Gender and Cultural Politics*. Boston: South End Press, 1999.

——. *Salvation: Black People and Love*. New York: Harper Perennial, 2001.

———. *Teaching Community: A Pedagogy of Hope.* New York: Routledge, 2003.

———. *We Real Cool: Black Men and Masculinity.* New York: Routledge, 2004.

———. *Belonging: A Culture of Place.* New York: Routledge, 2008.

hooks, bell, and West, Cornel. *Breaking Bread: Insurgent Black Intellectual Life.* Boston: South End Press, 1991.

Hunter, Margaret, and Nettles, Kimberly. "What About White Women?: Racial Politics in a Women's Studies Classroom." *American Sociological Association, 27* (October 1999): 385–397.

"In Depth with bell hooks." CSPAN Video Library. Available at http://www.c-spanvideo.org/program/InDepthw

Jackson III, Ronald. *Scripting the Black Masculine Body: Identity, Discourse, and Racial Politics in Popular Media.* Albany: SUNY Press, 2006.

Jhally, Sut, and Lewis, Justin. *Enlightened Racism: The Cosby Show, Audiences, and the Myth of the American Dream.* Boulder: Westview, 1992.

Johnson, Julia, Rich, Mark, and Castelan Cargile, Aaron. "'Why Are You Shoving This Stuff Down Our Throats?': Preparing Intercultural Educators to Challenge Performances of White Racism." *Journals of International and Intercultural Communication, 1* (May 2008): 113.

Jones, Bradley, and Mukherjee, Roopali. "From California to Michigan: Race, Rationality and Neoliberal Governmentality." *Communication and Critical/Cultural Studies,* 7 (2010): 401–422.

Joseph, Ralina L. "*'Hope Is Finally Making a Comeback':* First Lady Reframed," *Communication, Culture and Critique, 4,* no. 1 (2011): 56–77.

———. "'Tyra Banks Is Fat': Reading (Post-) Racism and (Post-) Feminism in the New Millennium." *Critical Studies in Media Communication, 26,* no. 3 (2009): 237–254.

Kahaney, Phyllis, and Liu, Judith, eds. *Contested Terrain: Diversity, Writing & Knowledge.* Ann Arbor: University of Michigan Press, 2001.

Kang, Jerry. "Trojan Horses of Race," *Harvard Law Review, 118,* no. 6 (2005): 1489–1593.

Kelly, Robin. *Yo' Mama's Dysfunktional! Fighting the Culture Wars in Urban America.* Boston: Beacon Street Press, 1998.

Lind, Rebecca Ann, ed. *Race/Gender/Class/Media: Considering Media Diversity Across Audiences, Content and Producers,* 3rd edition. New York: Prentice Hall, 2012.

Livingstone, Sonia. "Engaging with Media—A Matter of Literacy?" Keynote presentation, *Transforming Audiences: Identity/Creativity/Everyday Life.* University of Westminster, UK (2007), 4–5. Available at http://eprints.lse.ac.uk/2763/

Lowens, Randy. "How Do You Practice Intersectionality? An Interview with bell hooks." *Common Struggle,* 2009. Available at http://nefac.net/bellhooks

Mahiri, Jabari, and Conner, Erin. "Black Youth Violence Has a Bad Rap." *Journal of Social Issues, 59,* no. 1 (2003): 121–140.

Marable, Manning. *Race, Reform and Rebellion: The Second Reconstruction and Beyond in Black America, 1945–2006.* 3rd ed. Jackson: University Press of Mississippi, 2007.

Means Coleman, Robin R. *African American Viewers and the Black Situation Comedy: Situating Racial Humor.* New York: Garland, 1998.

———. ed. *Say It Loud! African American Audiences, Media and Identity.* New York: Routledge, 2002.

———. "The Gentrification of 'Black' in Black Popular Culture in the New Millennium." *Popular Communication, 4:* 79–94.

Mills, C. Wright. *The Sociological Imagination.* New York: Oxford Univerity Press, 1959.

———. "On Knowledge and Power." Reprinted in *Power, Politics and People: The Collected Essays of C. Wright Mills,* edited by I. L. Horowitz. New York: Oxford University Press, 1963.

Modood, Tariq. "Is Multiculturalism dead?" *Public Policy Research,* June–August (2008): 84–88.

Mulvey, Laura. "Visual Pleasure and Narrative Cinema," *Screen, 16,* no. 3 (1975): 6–18.

Nakamura, Lisa, and Chow-White, Peter, eds. *Race After the Internet.* New York: Routledge, 2011.

Olsen, Gary. "bell hooks and the Politics of Literacy: A Conversation." *Journal of Advanced Composition, 14,* (1994): 1–19.

Ono, Kent A. "Critical: A Finer Edge." *Communication and Critical/Cultural Studies, 8,* no. 1 (2011): 93–96.

Ono, Kent, and Pham, Vincent. *Asian Americans and Media.* New York: Polity Press, 2009.

Osbourne, Gwendolyn. "Women Who Look Like Me: Cultural Identity and Reader Responses to African American Romance Novels," in *Race/Gender/Media: Considering Diversity Across Audiences, Content and Producers,* 2nd ed., edited by Rebecca Ann Lind, 65–72. New York: Allyn & Bacon, 2010.

Owens, Debbie A. "Media Messages, Self-Identity and Race Relations," in *Say It Loud! African American Audiences Media and Identity,* edited by Robin R. Means Coleman, 77–93. New York: Routledge, 2002.

Pateman, Carol. *The Disorder of Women: Democracy, Feminism and Political Theory.* Stanford University Press, 1989.

Pierce-Baker, Charlotte. "A Quilting of Voices: Diversifying the Curriculum/Canon in the Humanities." *College Literature, 17,* no. 2 (1990): 152–161.

Putnam, Robert. *Bowling Alone: The Collapse and Revival of American Community.* New York: Simon & Schuster, 2001.

Ramsey, Eric. "Somehow, Learning to Live: On Being Critical." *Communication and Critical/Cultural Studies, 8,* no. 1 (2011), 90–92.

Rassulo, Michelle Miller, and Hecht, Michael L. "Performance As Persuasion: Trigger Scripting As a Tool for Education and Persuasion." *Literature in Performance, 8,* no.2 (1988). 51.

Rodgers, Daniel T. *Age of Fracture.* Cambridge: Belknap Press, 2011.

Roediger, David. "White Workers, New Democrats, and Affirmative Action." In *The House That Race Built,* edited by Wahneema Lubiano, 48–65. New York: Vintage, 1998.

Schiappa, Edward I. *Beyond Representational Correctness: Rethinking Criticism of Popular Media.* Albany: SUNY Press, 2008.

Squires, Catherine R. "Re-thinking the Black Public Sphere: An Alternative Vocabulary for Multiple Public Spheres," *Communication Theory, 12* (2002): 446–468.

———. *African Americans and the Media.* New York: Polity Press, 2010.

Stanley, Christine. "Coloring the Academic Landscape: Faculty of Color Breaking the Silence in Predominantly White Colleges and Universities," *American Educational Research Journal, 43,* no. 4 (2006 Winter): 701–736.

Trainor, Jennifer S. "'My Ancestors Didn't Own Slaves': Understanding White Talk About Race." *National Council of Teachers of English, 40* (2005): 140–167.

TuSmith, Bonnie, and Reddy, Maureen T., eds. *Race in the College Classroom: Pedagogy and Politics.* Rutgers University Press, 2002.

Vavrus, Mary. *Postfeminist News: Political Women in Media Culture.* Albany: SUNY Press, 2002.

Ward, Monique L. "'Wading Through the Stereotypes' Positive and Negative Associations Between Media Use and Black Adolescents' Conception of Self." *Developmental Psychology, 40,* no. 2 (2007): 84–94.

White, E. Francis. "The Price of Success," *The Women's Review of Books, 21,* no. 1 (October 2003): 17–18.

Young, Iris Marion. *Justice and the Politics of Difference.* Princeton: Princeton University Press, 1990.

Index

A CRITICAL INTRODUCTION TO MEDIA AND COMMUNICATION THEORY

David W. Park
Series Editor

The study of the media in the field of communication suffers from no shortage of theoretical perspectives from which to analyze media, messages, media systems, and audiences. One of the field's strengths has been its flexibility as it incorporates social scientific and humanist ideas in pursuit of a better understanding of communication and the media. This flexibility and abundance of ideas threaten to muddle the study of communication as it stakes out an interdisciplinary identity.

This series puts on center stage individuals and ideas whose importance to the study of communication can be reconfigured, reinvented, and refocused. Each of the specially commissioned books in the series shares a concern for the history of theory in the field of communication. Books provide sophisticated discussions of the relevance of particular theorists or theories, with an emphasis on re-inventing the field of communication, whether by incorporating ideas often considered to be 'outside' the field or by providing fresh analyses of ideas that have long been considered vital in the field's past. Though theoretical in focus, the books are at all times concerned with the applicability of theory to empirical research and experience and are designed to be accessible, yet critical, for students—undergraduates and postgraduates—and scholars.

For additional information about this series or for the submission of manuscripts, please contact:

David W. Park
park@lakeforest.edu

To order other books in this series, please contact our Customer Service Department:

(800) 770-LANG (within the U.S.)
(212) 647-7706 (outside the U.S.)
(212) 647-7707 FAX

Or browse online by series:
www.peterlang.com